"I believe we are on the verge of developing a new kind of culture. ... in this culture it will be the child—and not the parent and grandparent—that represents what is to come."

- *Margaret Mead "Prefigurative Cultures and Unknown Children" (1973)*

EMPOWERED!

Re-framing 'Growing Up' for a New Age

A NEW '20-YEAR-TIME-HORIZON' VISION
of Growing Up in the World
FOR A NEW GENERATION OF HUMANS

---

by Marc Prensky

Ordering Information:
Special discounts are available on quantity purchases
by corporations, associations, and others. For details, contact
marcprensky@gmail.com

Published by EAI Press, an imprint of the Global Ministry
of Empowerment, Accomplishment & Impact
First Edition, 2022 ISBN 978-0-578-26140-9

Table of Contents

For Rie and Sky —
and for all the Empowered Humans to come

PART I

BECOMING EMPOWERED

Re-framing the Journey of Growing Up for a New Age

A 20-year-time horizon vision for the new generation of humans now growing up in the world

Chapter 1

RE-FRAMING
A NEW JOURNEY
FOR A
NEW GENERATION

From {a 20th century world}
To [a 21st century world]

AS WE START what many call the second millennium—really the 300th (approximately) for *homo sapiens*—all young humans are embarking on a new journey. That journey will be partly to space as more and more leave our planet. But there will be a new journey happening for young people here on Earth as well. I call it ***The New Journey to Empowerment***.

A 20-Year Trip

Unlike humans' journey to space, which may go on forever, I estimate that the journey to Empowerment will take around 20 years— the time for the people born in the 21st century to grow up and take the world into their own hands. This book is about our next generation, their increasing capabilities, and where they are likely to be around the year 2040 or so—if we don't block their way.

We desperately need to look at this 20-year horizon, because today most adults are focused on a far shorter time frame, e.g., what happens to our children in the next few years, or, at most, the 10-year horizon of the United Nations' Sustainable Development Goals and the OECD. But it is important for our children's sake that we also focus on a somewhat longer (but still foreseeable) term—in a way few are currently doing. I hope this book will help.

The Change is in Empowerment

Except here and there, our world is unlikely to have changed dramatically on the surface in 20 years. Most homes and buildings from the past will still exist, along with some new ones.

But in 20 years there will be enormously new capabilities underneath—stemming from changes that have already begun in technology, infrastructure, and more.

It is likely that in 20 years most of the adults alive today will not have changed dramatically either. Those individuals, all born in the 20th century, may be somewhat healthier, and may have some new opportunities. Most, however, will retain their 20th century attitudes and beliefs.

Yet underneath them a new, and different generation is rising. The capabilities of these rising humans, who have arrived into the world since the start of the 21st century, will be, by 2040, dramatically increased. Overall, they will be far more empowered to accomplish and to change things positively in their world. This new generation of humans, suddenly empowered in a new, bottom-up way, will begin to make enormous positive change in the world.

It is this new empowerment of the world's young people over the next 20 years—and the positive changes it will bring—that is the subject of this book. By 2040, these empowered, 21st-century-born people will comprise more than half of humanity. The results will, I believe, be profound.

Hold on…

"Wait—aren't humans already empowered?" you might ask. "After all, we have come to completely dominate our planet—to the point of being able to destroy everything on it. Isn't that empowerment enough?"

Perhaps, but that it is not the kind of empowerment I am talking about. Certainly humanity, through the 20th century, in various groups and combinations, has done many powerful things, both positive and negative.

But very few *individual* humans—especially young humans—have had much power over all that time. Most have lives that are controlled by others—first by parents, then by schools, and then by employers and the vicissitudes of life. Most individual humans, up until now, just survived as long as they could—or didn't. Some joined larger groups. Some had various kinds of careers.

Despite Margaret Mead's famous pronouncement: "Never doubt that a small group of committed individuals can change the world—it's the only thing that ever has," up until now a stunningly small number of the billions of humans that have ever existed have made a difference—as individuals—to humanity. According to one researcher, out of the roughly one hundred five billion humans who have ever lived, less than five thousand individuals are remembered by name in all the world's encyclopedias. [1]

Human empowerment happened through large groups—sparked, perhaps, by Mead's smaller ones and a few individuals. Mostly, humans have been a collection of hives. In the entire history of humankind very few individual people were empowered to do and accomplish positive things—and almost never starting when they were young (Mozart, and perhaps a few others, excepted.) Up until now, in order to accomplish useful things, most humans had to wait to grow up and become cogs in someone's larger machine.

That is Changing

Today, as we enter the New Age of Empowerment, this is already different. We see pre-teens creating devices that solve real environmental problems (Gitanjali Rao), teenagers beginning to organize the world's young people for change (Greta Thunberg), and 20-somethings start companies that have grown to among the biggest in the world (Google, Facebook, YouTube). They are the harbingers of what is coming.

There is a strange duality and tension, in humans, between individuals and groups. While we are all alike in a great many aspects, we are all also individuals, starting even before birth—each of whom sees the world from our own unique perspective, each of us searching, individually, for comfort and meaning.

We form, and benefit from, groups and cultures. But each individual counts—above all—to him or herself. Every one of us starts with personal dreams, and flourishes as those dreams get realized. They get realized, often, through group action, yet everything the world that is human-made began as an idea in the mind of a single individual.

Few, in this duality, have been able to realize their individual dreams, and those who were lucky enough to do so typically had to wait for adulthood. *Now they don't have to wait.* They can begin to realize dreams in the world—and show positive results—from the earliest ages. For young humans it is a new age and a new journey: a Journey to Empowerment.

Pessimism or Optimism?

In the so-called 20th century, the global human population grew from under 2 billion to over 8 billion. That population has split, economically, into two groups: an extremely small wealthy and powerful "club" (in multiple senses of that term), and "everyone else." Given the growth of technology—which was partly the cause of the split—the question of what will happen to that "everyone else" is increasingly on people's minds. A growing number are pessimistic: Some see technology taking over. Many worry about the working class disappearing. Some even foresee a huge useless class of humans forming on the globe that will have to somehow be supported—or not— because they can't support themselves.

I See Things Differently

I don't see it like that. Certainly A.I. (artificial intelligence) and automation are coming quickly and are going to change things radically. But even with widespread A.I. and automation—*and no matter how large the population grows*—

Humanity will *never* run out of dreams to realize, problems to fix, people who need help, or people who want to help them.

The Journey to Empowerment is about the coming billions of humans finding they now have the power to do those things, and

about their using that power— starting at the youngest age
in small teams—for the good of the world.

Framing a New World, and A New Process of Growin

Because today's adults—all 20th century-born—grew
world where those still being "raised" had almost no powe
the New Journey to Empowerment begins with today's
people. A key part of starting their new journey is a re-fran
how those young people—21st century humans—see the wor
live in. Far more profoundly than most adults realize, th
already a very different world from the 20th century, wl
today's adults grew up—and they know it.

A great many young people (along with some, but fewer,
have begun to understand how fast the world in changing, a
a "new process of growing up" is required for individuals to
in their new and different world of the mid-to-late 21st century
though, as yet, most young people are unable to articulate tl
some cases, adults *are* helping young people build this new gr
up process, as science gains new knowledge about humans'
years and how to shape them.

But when adults are *not* offering positive help in designing
process—and in most cases they are not—the young people a
to design it on their own. And, in fact, they already are. Tl
framing that they are already doing for their new world, and th
shall see, includes how they—i.e., 21st century young people—

- their coming times,
- who they are,
- what they believe,
- what their world will be like,
- what they should aspire to,

13

- what is universal for all of them,
- what they are called,
- and the whole process of how they go from birth to adulthood—what is generally called "growing up"

in and for their own times and new Age.

This book is about describing this re-framing and the young people's new journey—at least as it appears to me. I will discuss what I see as the different ways young people are beginning to see the world and changes in the various "phases" of growing up that I see coming. I will show how young peoples' beliefs are changing—in ways that lead to new humans being far more empowered than they were in the past. The "New Journey to Empowerment" has several stages, and to get there, all these stages will need to work in sync.

To Empowerment *from* Where?

As our young people move to empowerment, it is worth asking "from where do they start?"—particularly from their (i.e., from the young people's) point of view.

I believe our young people are finally about to leave a very long period characterized, mainly, by *control*—both by parents and schools—and, particularly recently, of considerable floundering. Despite adults' sometimes-offered opinions that both these things are "good for them," neither control nor floundering are things most young people enjoy.

Many of the coming changes are so profound and different that they are difficult, in many cases, for the current adult generation to accept. Today's adults are, in a deep sense, the last in their line. All of them were born, and most grew up, grew up in the 20th century, before the Internet and digital technology fully entered human life.

Today's adults are the "Last Pre-Internet Generation" the world will ever know. Today's young people, as I foresaw 20 years ago are the first true "digital natives."

ALL Dreams—Not just Some

In the new world they are growing up in, I believe these Digital Natives will be able to do much better, starting much earlier.

I believe, strongly, that this is true for all of them—not just for those who have the most immediate access to new technology. The technology may still be coming for many, *but the dreams are already there.*

It bears remembering—and repeating—that *all* young people start with dreams—a great many of which get crushed as they grow up. Now for the first time in history, all those young people are becoming empowered to realize those dreams, to a far greater extent than ever in the past. Those dreams may include, *but do not require* having technology—at least not first.

This does *not* mean every person who happens to be young will achieve dreams of becoming rich or become a rock star. ***But it DOES mean that people who happen to be young are now getting the power, while they are still young, to make their world a better place in ways they can imagine.*** This was not generally possible in the past.

Bringing Out, Not Putting In

The new frame is, overall, in at least one important respect *totally opposite* from the old, 20th century frame. The old frame of growing up was all about putting things *INTO* young people, including beliefs, culture, history, knowledge and more. We spent so much time doing that that—and then testing whether our inputs

15

got in—that we hardly ever listened or cared about what was coming out. Essentially, we tramped down, and often extinguished, the output and imagination of a huge portion of our people—the young—all their young lives because we thought they had nothing to contribute until we shaped them to our ways and purposes. And then, when they grew up, we complained about their lack of imagination!

The New Age of Empowerment is less about putting things into people, and more about bringing out what is already there. This graphic illustrates and underscores the change:

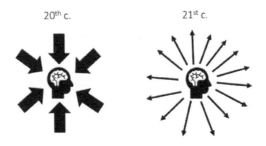

One sad result of our old frame is an "imagination crisis"— of our own making. I believe the only way our children will have a decent chance in the future *is to get that imagination back*. The New Journey to Empowerment is all about liberating and unleashing young people's imagination and applying it to real-world accomplishment—with impact.

Reframing Needed

In order to for us to liberate imagination, make the journey, and get to the end we need (Empowerment), it is necessary for people—both young and old—to see the world in new ways. I call these new ways "**re-framings**." Re-framings are what this book is about.

These are the re-framings I will be talking about in the coming chapters:

REFRAMING	FROM	TO
Our young people's times	4th Industrial Revolution	New Age of Empowerment
Who young people are	Humans with Tools	Symbiotic Human Hybrids
Where Young People Will Live	Earth and Imagination	Earth, Imagination & Cloud
What young people believe	Old, 20th Century Beliefs	New, 21st Century Beliefs
Young people's future world	A World of Experience	A New Frontier of Exploration
Young people's aspirations	Generational Replacement	Continuous Invention
What's universal for young people	Academic Success	Real-World Accomplishment
Young people's labels	Children, Kids, Students, Learners	PEOPLE—who happen to be young
Young people's journey of growing up	Being Directed	Becoming Empowered
- Parenting	Ownership	Empowerment
- Learning	An End in Itself	A Means for Accomplishing
- School Years	Schools	Empowerment Hubs
- Curriculum	Courses & Classes	Projects
- Basics	The Old Artifacts	Meeting New Needs
- Skills	Basic, Hard/Soft, 21st Century	Task-specifics & Transferable Capabilities
- Assessment	Grades, Ranking, Degrees	Before & After, Measurable Positive Impact
- Work	Jobs	Adding Unique Value to Projects

As we re-frame our young people's world, we will be using a "map" to see where we are on the Journey to Empowerment:

'THE MAP'

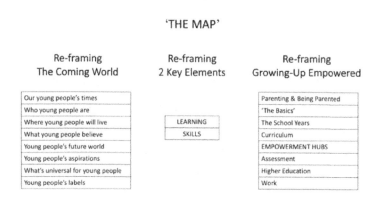

The Elements of Empowerment

But before we start on our journey of re-framing, I want to highlight four elements that I consider the *basic needs* for empowerment, so that you can keep them in mind as you read. They are:

- New, Empowering **BELIEFS**
- Real-World **ACCOMPLISHMENT**
- Technology & Team **SYMBIOSIS**
- Self-knowledge and applied **UNIQUENESS**

We will consider each of them—and its implications, as we move forward.

I want to also introduce, and highlight, two additional features. At the end of each chapter I offer *"Harbingers"* of the coming changes I describe. These are short vignettes of people I have met who are in advance of their time, and have helped inspire my future thinking. Each chapter also concludes with a question or questions for you to reflect on.

Here are the first of these:

Harbingers

Two well-known participants on the journey that is coming are Elon Musk (from the old generation), and Greta Thunberg (from the new one). Musk is already in many ways what Greta will, I believe, become. Seen in terms of the four elements of empowerment above, Greta and Elon *both* have empowering beliefs—they know where they want the future to go. Both have accomplished much in order to get there. Both are unique.

An important difference, though, is that Elon is already much more symbiotic with technology than is Greta. While Greta has big goals (mitigating climate change), she hasn't yet figured out, as I write, how to use many of the resources now at her disposal to accomplish them. Elon not only has huge goals (mass electric cars, reusable rockets, going to Mars) but he is *already* employing every symbiotic technological extension he has to accomplish them. Greta and her generation will, I predict, soon figure out how to do this, and follow.

Reflection Questions

In what fundamental ways do you think the world of our children will be different from ours? Are adults' fears of this coming world realistic, or are they unfounded or overblown? Most importantly, are our fear-induced behaviors stopping our young people from getting there faster?

PART II

RE-FRAMING THE 21ST CENTURY WORLD

Chapter 2

SEEING THINGS IN A NEW WAY

From {20th Century Frames}
to [21st Century Frames]

WE ALL KNOW THESE ARE VERY TRANSITIONAL TIMES FOR HUMANITY—even if we don't know exactly what we are transitioning to. The question I ask in this book is

---

How can we—and the rising generations—re-frame these times for maximum helpfulness?

One reason we require new frames is that for the generations now rising, the pace of change has dramatically speeded up. A great deal new is emerging, and the world is experiencing much upheaval—even as a great deal continues as before, that many from previous generations cling to.

This raises many questions: What *should* continue? What should be abandoned? What replaced? How do we decide? How do we even think about it? Today a great many are confused or conflicted about this. This is just the kind of situation in which re-framing what we see can be very useful.

Seeing in A New Way

A "frame" is our *choice* of how we see the world. Pictures such as the one above that can be viewed in two ways, and the proverbial half-full or half-empty glass, are but tiny examples of our making these framing choices.

A frame is the "lens" we choose to look through as we consider the future—it is our choice of the perspective we think will be most helpful to our understanding. In Thomas Kuhn's terms [2], a frame is the "paradigm" we decide to adopt and accept. "Mindsets," "beliefs" and "worldviews" are other names some use for frames.

Much in our lives depends on the frames we adopt—the perspective we choose to take. The element of choice is very important. Some may think there is only one objective way to see the world. "But," neuroscientists Eric C. Anderson and Lisa Feldman Barrett remind us, while "people believe they experience the world objectively [...] research continually demonstrates that beliefs influence perception."

In other words, frames matter. A lot.

Both How We See and How We Are Seen

A usual way of looking at frames is "How we see the world." This generally includes, metaphorically, both the picture frame we put around the world and the lenses through which we see it.

We can also re-frame the "frames metaphor" to include *how we are seen by other people*. This is like focusing on the plastic or metal that *holds* the lenses in the eyeglasses on our face. Others can perceive us (and we can perceive others) as wearing—i.e., having—a particular frame, or set of frames (i.e., our belief sets about the world, religious and more)—and that influences our behavior towards each other. Anyone who has ever chosen eyeglass or sunglass frames knows just how many frame choices there are—we often own several pairs, for different occasions, depending on how we want to be perceived.

But while it is easy to change our *outside* look, from our *inner* perspective—i.e., the lenses we see each the world through, there is typically only one prescription at a time that is right for us—the framing that makes the world most clear to *our* eyes.

Our Frames Are Our Choice

Our physical eyes and vision are shaped by nature, individually and differently in each case, and often necessitating correction to see clearly. There is a clear physical definition of "seeing clearly," and the optician's job is to find it.

The metaphorical frames we are talking about here occur, rather, in our minds, in ways we do not yet fully understand. Yet one thing is very clear—when it comes to mental lenses and frames, *we get to choose*—just as we get to pick our eyeglass frames. There is no one prescription that is "clinically right." The frame we choose reflects many factors—often including where and how we grew up, such as with a regional, cultural, or religious frame. And it may go beyond that as well, to individual preferences.

In certain well-known optical illusions—such as the young [woman / old hag] shown above or the well-known [profiles / vase]—most can only see one frame at a time, not both. This appears to be true for mental frames as well. We may, or may not, know both exist, but at any moment we believe only one to be true—the one we have chosen our own. It is hard for a person to hold two opposing frames simultaneously—it causes conflict, or dissonance, in our minds. Perhaps to avoid this conflict, our mental frames—i.e., our deeply-held beliefs about how the world works—do not change easily or frequently.

The "Aha" Moment

Yet our choice of frame can change instantly when someone shows us, or we discover, a better one—I call this an "aha" moment (some call it an "epiphany.") Even during the slow-changing times of the past humans experienced a number of these collective epiphanies—i.e., group re-frames about the world. ("Aha," some may have said when Magellan arrived home, "the world is round and not flat! That makes so much more sense!")

Some of these aha's resulted from better tools or more complete or precise observations, such as the re-frame of the earth's being a sphere and not flat, or the re-frame of the planet's traveling around the sun and not the Earth. Other re-frames, such as re-framing to the sovereignty of the people rather than of hereditary kings, or from many gods to a single God, were the result of societal changes.

Typically, re-framings happen inside people's minds, without any outward manifestations. Some groups, though, do employ signs—distinctive clothing or body markings—to visibly indicate the frame inside. These are, metaphorically, the "glasses frames" we spoke of earlier—i.e., the frame in which we want the world to perceive us.

"Muscle Memory"

Changing one's frames is crucial for making changes in behavior—the beliefs represented by our frames determine everything we do or don't do. But while frame change is a required first step, just changing one's frame(s) doesn't necessarily, by itself, lead to behavior change. Our behavior in an old frame often becomes automatic—some refer to this, metaphorically, as "muscle memory." [4] Neuroscientists sometimes call it "zombie" behavior. [5] At times we have gotten so accustomed to doing something in a particular way that *even when our beliefs change* we still do the old things—*knowing they are wrong or ineffective*. This so-called "muscle memory" in humans plays a large part in preventing needed changes from taking place. Education—where many practitioners already agree they are not doing the right thing for their students— is one of the prime examples.

What people in that position need, I believe, is *a clear vision of what they can do instead*. That is something I hope to provide in this book.

Re-frames Can Take Time

Some re-framing takes a long time to be widely accepted. Today, we are in the middle of the kind of "crisis" period that Thomas Kuhn says comes (in his famous book *The Structure of Scientific Revolution* [6]) whenever we are changing frames. (Kuhn calls frames "paradigms.") Humans are now finding many of our old frames, beliefs, paradigms, and worldviews don't fit the new world we are entering. Today the world is currently going through a process of re-framing a great many things in our lives—at different speeds in different places. For example, the world is only partly through a re-frame that skin color in people, like paint color in cars, doesn't really matter. Humans are also going through re-frames about how we view women, same sex couples, physical and sexual abusers, individuals who are LGBTQ+, and many other things. People generally accept new frames gradually, as they see they make more sense, and are more useful explanations of their world. All the world's big re-frames took hold because they were more useful in some way.

In order to fully understand our changing world additional re-frames are needed—and they are coming, as we will see throughout this book. One of the biggest, I believe, is changing the world's frame regarding young people. That is what this book, in its essence, is about. It is also why we need to think on a 20-year time horizon—that is the amount of time it will take for this new generation, with its different beliefs, to rise to adulthood.

How Re-framing Can Help

One of the best examples of how re-framing can help comes from the work of Carol Dweck.[7] She has suggested students reframe how they see themselves—from having a "fixed mindset" to having a "Growth Mindset." This re-frame alone changes, in a positive way, how many behave. An entrepreneurial coach, Peter Diamandis, offers his own collection of alternative "mindsets" to budding entrepreneurs—regarding Abundance, Exponential Growth, Longevity and more—to help entrepreneurs act differently in building businesses. [8]

Why Re-frame?

Re-framing is useful—and often required—to make the world clearer and more understandable—particularly in times of change. Re-frames can be seen as *alternative stories or narratives* that we choose to tell ourselves and accept about how the world is and how it works. They are "updates" of the "shared myths," described by Yuval Noah Harari [9], that help large groups of people move in common directions.

For example, when natural disasters hurt communities deeply a re-frame to seeing a "divine being" as controlling them for its own unknown purposes, rather than their just being random, can be very helpful. When fossils and other evidence indicating progressive changes in various species are discovered, a re-frame by scientists regarding how the world came into being—from "God created" to "natural selection"—may be more useful to them.

People often tend to seek out others with the same frames. This is partly what leads to cultures.

Criteria for Re-framing

The best criteria for choosing a frame are *usefulness* and *helpfulness* (although these are not always the ones used.) Frames are best seen not as "right" or "wrong" but rather as more, or less, helpful and useful. The "lenses" through which we choose to look at the world are part of our self-definition. Each of us can, and does, choose the frame(s) we use.

In essence, re-framing is just looking at, or seeing, the same things differently. A re-frame can be just a change in perspective, such as putting a positive, rather than a negative spin on some thing or event (e.g., seeing the glass as half- full rather than half-empty). The world was famously re-framed for singer Elton John by his continually wearing rose-colored glasses. (This does, indeed, make the world look "rosier." I recommend trying it, at least once.)

Big re-frames, such as "the earth being a globe," or the "growth mindset," or "abundance, not scarcity," can open up whole new options and worlds, and lead to very different actions on our part.

Many people in the world, as I write, are currently going through a re-framing from "we seem to be going through a hot spell" to "the global climate is changing." Others resist adopting this new frame. It remains to be seen how far this re-framing will go and what actions it will lead to.

I See New Frames Often

As I look the world, and the way others have framed it, re-frames frequently occur to me. Whenever most are looking at the world in one way, I am inspired to try to look at it in another. Seeking a new perspective has always been more helpful to me than going incrementally further in the same direction.

I thank the Boston Consulting Group, and my 6 years there, for helping develop my ability to do large-scale re-framing of whole industries. Here I'm trying to apply some of this to humanity and our times.

Re-framing doesn't always produce useful results—but it very often does. In the search for new solutions, it is always worth a try.

Digital Natives

Of all the re-frames I've ever done over my life, the one that is known and useful to the most people is my classifying of humans, around the turn of the millennium, as "Digital Natives" and "Digital Immigrants." A great many criticized this framing as an over-generalization, and found reasons to question it. But the frame has stuck around—most likely because it contains a useful and helpful nugget of truth.

Around the year 2000, as I watched the young people working in my company at that time, I began to see new generational changes in a new way—not just as the old, traditional process of youth rebellion, but as *something new and different*—something for which people—especially parents—didn't have a good explanation, or "frame." In an article in *On the Horizon,* [10] an obscure online journal, I re-framed these young people as "digital natives" (i.e., native speakers of the digital language) and their parents as "digital immigrants," (i.e., people who had learned "digital" as a second language.) Little did I know at the time the impact this re-frame would have.

Nothing besides the new names I gave the generations— i.e., the frame—actually changed. But you can tell a new frame is helpful when people start using it, and don't stop. Today, two decades later, the terms Digital Natives and Digital Immigrants still show up daily around the world in stories and headlines. They have entered the English lexicon and can be found in the Oxford English Dictionary. I am sure those words will show up on my tombstone, should I have one. :)

Additional Re-frames

This book is about a number of additional re-frames, lenses, and perspectives that have occurred to me in the two decades since. I have found all of them helpful in making sense of the coming world of the mid-to-late 21st century, i.e., the world into which today's young people are growing up. I hope they are helpful to you as well.

New Frames

In each of the chapters of the book I present a number of re-frames that I think are useful for better understanding and for dealing with the mid-to-late 21st century—the time in which our children and grandchildren will live. You might find some of them more "radical" than others. But my hope is that all of them will help you consider what's coming in a different way. What you do with that is entirely up to you. (Should you agree with *all* of them, I want to know who you are!)

Structure

Within a larger, overall re-framing of "A New Age of Empowerment," I will try to re-frame Who Young People Are, Where They Live, Their Beliefs, Their Needs, Their Future, What's Universal for them, What they are Called, How they Grow Up, Their Skills, Their Curricula, Learning, Work, and even their view of Humanity.

And all in under 280 pages!

My guess is that some of these new re-frames will be unsettling, and even disturbing to you. Some of the most radical include seeing humans as becoming symbiotic with technology, seeing learning as no longer the main goal for young people, and seeing reading, writing and arithmetic as no longer the basics all future young people need. My goal is not just to provoke you (although I hope I do!), but to *give you new and different perspectives to think about*. I hope, as you read, you will concur with what I consider the highest praise I ever get: "He made me think differently!"

At the end of each chapter I will include "*Harbingers*"—short vignettes of people who have inspired my re-framings, and I conclude each chapter with questions for you to reflect on.

Let's start!

But Wait...

But before we begin, I offer you an option.

I begin the book with the overall, general picture of how things are changing, but *you* may be particularly interested in the *implications* of that picture, i.e., the specific re-frames I offer for our young people's "growing up." That includes the implications of the New Age of Empowerment for learning, the school years, curricula, basics, skills, assessment, parenting, and work. If you seek this information first, you can go directly to those implications—which comprise Parts III and IV of this book—by turning now to either Chapter 11 (*Re-framing Learning*), or Part IV (*Re-framing the 21st Century Journey of Growing Up Empowered.*)

If that's not what you need immediately, then let us begin with the overall picture, by re-framing the times in which all our young people will live—either already today, or within their lifetimes.

Harbingers

Among the many school-age teams I find particularly interesting are:

(1) a class of 3-year-olds in Spain who designed—and got their town mayor to install—lower waste bins on city poles (https://youtu.be/5u1cCbSYh2Q); and

(2) a team of middle school girls in Georgia (U.S.A.) The girls not only 3D-printed prosthetic hands, but reached out as well via social media to find young people who needed them. (https://youtu.be/XQ8tPOqN7WE&t=26s) Details on these two teams—

and over 100 other young people and teams who are harbingers of what is to come—can be found at https://btwdatabase.org.

Reflection Question

If you have previously heard of my (now 20-year-old) reframing of today's young people as Digital Natives, and their parents as Digital Immigrants, was this reframing helpful to you? Why or why not? Have you done any re-framing of your own?

Chapter 3

RE-FRAMING OUR YOUNG PEOPLE'S TIMES

From {The "4th Industrial Revolution"}
to [The New Age of Empowerment]

LET'S START by thinking about ways to re-frame the time period (or "Age") our young people are currently entering into and will be fully part of in 20 years: the mid-to-late 21st century. To begin, we might ask "What's different?" For me, one of the most important differences is worldwide connection of young people starting at a very young age.

We are currently in the process of transitioning

From the Last Pre-Internet Generation the world will ever know,

To the world's first Internet Generation.

That change, along with all the other technological changes that have accompanied it, right around the year 2000, has huge implications for our young people.

So how can we most usefully frame their time?

Re-naming

Sometimes useful re-framing can come purely through re-naming—as with "Digital Natives." Several names have already suggested to re-frame the new period into which our children are quickly moving.

Some call the New Age "The Fourth Industrial Revolution"—employing a business evolution frame. Others—employing a major influence frame—call it "The Anthropocene," meaning The Age of Human Domination. Some—using a frame of technological risk and disruption—are working to frame it as a time that is more Human-Centric than machine-centric. Still others—framing the times around exponentially advancing technology—call it an "Age of Abundance." I'm sure there are more.

Trying on each of these frames and seeing the world through each of their different lenses is a useful exercise that I recommend doing. In the end, after trying them all, we will each chose the frame that is most helpful and useful to us.

My Preferred Re-Frame

But if helpfulness and usefulness are indeed the criteria for choosing a frame, it seems to me that framing our times around human domination, or business, or even technology alone, is not the most useful way to go. Rather, the overall frame I find most helpful for our coming times, and that I suggest we use, is one of *increasing empowerment—especially empowerment of our young people.* That frame is positive for all—for humans, for business, for technology and for all of society—particularly if the new power is used in positive ways. Empowering our young people will, of course, eventually empower *all* humans.

And the *all* is important—it is not helpful to leave some people out. I believe the relationship of *all* young people to the world is about to change in these new times. Here is the 21st century frame I find most helpful.

We are moving:

> *From a time where young people had little or no power,*
>
> **To a time when young humans have far more power to accomplish in the world than they ever had before in history.**

Name That Frame

Because a new frame requires a way to call it and refer to it, I call this fast-arriving time

> *The New Age of Empowerment*
> *for people growing up.*

The New Age begins with the empowerment of those people who happen to be—and I would say are lucky to be—young at the start of the second millennium. As we will see in detail in the next chapter, they are all now becoming *Symbiotically Empowered Humans.*

A New Frontier

I often ask people I meet, both young and old, if they are afraid of the future, and a great many say yes. "Fear is the dominant emotion of our time," says business consultant John Hagel. [11]

One reason people are afraid is that the New Age of Empowerment is, metaphorically, a *new frontier* for humanity. I explore this "frontier" metaphor further in Chapter 5. But let me note for now that whenever any new frontier opens, it is normal for many people to fear going there. Despite humans' so-called "spirit of exploration" or "adventure," I believe most humans crave *comfort* above all else (beyond just staying alive). A new frontier is not, typically, comfortable.

So, a great many of today's adults are already uncomfortable in, and afraid of, entering this new world we are approaching—and are particularly fearful of sending their children into it. Adults, after all, are tasked with protecting their young from harm.

Most adults don't go any farther into the new frontier than they have to, and they often try hard to keep their children out of it—for example by not letting their children get connected online at young ages, or by limiting the time their children spend with their devices, or by taking away those devices at bedtimes or at classroom doors. Many adults think that by controlling their children's behaviors they are "protecting" the children—whom they know have already, in most cases, crossed the frontier.

Afraid? Or Excited!

But how useful is it to our young people for adults to frame the coming age as a time to be feared? Of course there are many unknowns. And there are, clearly, some potential big issues—including the possibilities of our planet's climate no longer supporting humans, and of nuclear self-annihilation of our species. But I am enough of an optimist to think those dangers will be overcome.

My strong sense is that fear is an inappropriate frame for our young people's future. I think it will be far more useful and helpful to young people to re-frame their future, far more positively and hopefully, in terms of empowerment. I think we can relax—and rejoice in the fact that our newly-empowered young people will find the means to deal with their fast-changing environment and rapidly approaching crises.

Further, I strongly believe it is unnecessary to protect young people from the new frontier—despite potential danger—because *being there is how they learn to adjust and cope.* Plus, it is often, for them—in some cases *because* of the possible danger—an exciting place to be. Any harm will come, I believe, from preventing our young people from going in as deeply as they want to, even at early ages. Even though keeping their own, or others' children out may, in fact, give adults some short-term comfort, I believe we will all be better off if adults empower young people as much, and as quickly as possible.

What Does *'Empowering'* Young People Mean?

But what, exactly, does "empower them" mean? Many adults think they are already empowering young people. Some even think education—as we do it—is empowering for young people.

I strongly disagree, because the term *empowerment*, for me, has a very specific meaning:

Empowerment is SELF-DIRECTION plus
ACCOMPLISHMENT with IMPACT

If the people can't choose their own direction(s) to go in, ***and*** we can't actually see their accomplishment(s)—i.e., results with positive real-world impact—there is no empowerment.

Without that choice and impact, our young people are NOT empowered—*yet*. There may be "improvement" along some dimensions, or even an increase in "potential." But an increase in "potential," or "theoretical power to accomplish someday," is not, for me, empowerment.

Empowerment is rather the "actual demonstration of getting done useful things they want to in their world." Getting useful things done—and having impact—is something that the world's newly empowered young people are now capable of doing at a level far beyond what their parents or forebears were capable of at their age— no matter what that age may be.

The "judges" of usefulness and impact are the young people themselves and the communities in which they live. Combined with New Empowering Beliefs—which I will discuss in Chapter 3—this "empowerment through self-direction and accomplishment with impact" is what defines the New Age.

Will the New Age of Empowerment Hurt or Harm Young People, Or Help Them?

Many adults hesitate before wanting to empower their children in this sense of self-direction, real-world accomplishment, and new beliefs. Many cry "Wait—look at all the time they're spending with screens—we don't really know the all the consequences—maybe it's bad for them." Others say, "just let them be kids," meaning "don't give them responsibilities like we have—those will come later."

I believe most adults want to help young people. (Although sadly, it should be noted, we still have a world with child trafficking, kid-armies, and laws dictating where young people, whether they like it or not, must spend their day.) Certainly, no young person *wants* to be harmed.

But there is good news for those young people.

I think what "being a kid" and "growing up" means will be far different in the new Age of Empowerment—and much better. Play, for example, may still be important, but rather than just playing in the streets, or in their bedrooms, young people are now becoming empowered—through their play and otherwise—to voluntarily and happily have a positive impact on their world.

The bad news, however, is that adults are often willing to help only within their own, old, frame of "*unempowered kids.*" Too many adults are still willing to ban devices, limit screen time, force kids to study things they don't want to, and keep kids from what they imagine—not actually knowing much about them—as perils. One of my saddest memories is asking a high-school girl if she played videogames. "No," she answered, "my parents deprived me."

Do Our Children Need to Be Like Us?

I think a big reason we are willing to do these backward-looking things is that *we want our children to be like us.* We want them to live in our frame—and not to move to becoming something else.

But already, the young people of today—and certainly those of tomorrow—are NOT like us (i.e., like 20th century-born adults) in many fundamental ways. Although they may appear the same on the surface, they are no longer "little us's." Their capabilities and beliefs are changing rapidly and radically, along with their world—and re-framing on our part can help them move forward into that new world, as we will see.

Adults' who keep young people from their own future—even with the supposed justification that it is "for their own good"—*truly do harm to those young people* by holding them back. Rather than dragging our children back to the lives we thought (and may still think) are good—*even though we are worried, and even though we want to pass on to our children things we enjoyed in the past*—we should be trying to empower young people as quickly as possible to succeed in the new frontier that will be *their* life. That is why I think it is so useful to re-frame their times as a *New Age of Empowerment* for young people.

Reframing the Previous (20th) Century

In addition to re-framing the future, it is also useful to re-frame the past—i.e., to revise our perspective of the 20th century based on what we now know. Currently, I believe the most useful way to re-frame the 20th century—the time in which all today's adults were born—is as *having ended.*

Many 20th century people—particularly in certain places—saw their own times, or parts of those times, as being the best ever for humans—and want to preserve those parts as a legacy for their children. But as good as many of today's adults many think their century was, they are better off accepting and dealing with the fact that *their children are now in a new time.* My sense is that few, if any, young people have a desire to go back. Young people both want and need to live in their own times.

And the times, since the start of the 21st century, have changed both rapidly and radically. Our children now live—and will live— in an Age of Empowerment, coming fast to all, *and empowerment is what they should be expecting.* Without denigrating, in any way, the accomplishments of the people of the 20th century, those people are—as I said at the start—the last individually un-empowered generation the world will ever see. Today's young people—the first generation to grow up from birth with an Internet rather than dragging our young people back to the lives we thought (and may still think) are good —are the first generation of a New Age—an age of empowered young people.

Empower Them Now!

Remember, our criterion for a successful re-frame is usefulness. It is very useful to frame the period we are entering into as a *great time* for the people who have the good fortune to be young at this moment—i.e., at the start of the 21st century. Of course, some of these young people currently have less than others, in many ways, and we should help them catch up. But even the less fortunate—and *all* people alive today, if they want it—have huge new power in their hands to shape their world in a positive way.

Yet...

Yet as many young people are now finding out—including young activist Greta Thunberg—the new power will not be easily and generously handed over by adults. Nor will adults change their behaviors just because young people think differently. In many cases, power will need to be *seized* from the adults, who believe it is theirs—even when they are not doing a good job with it. Today's young people must *choose to* and *work to* deploy their new power for it to have maximum positive effect.

Any adults who want to help young people will do well to re-frame their own task from "protecting young people" to "empowering young people." If enough adults do this, the New Age of Empowerment will be a wonderful time for all of us. If not, the transition we spoke of at the start will be much more painful.

In the coming chapters we shall look more closely at who those newly-empowered young people are.

Harbingers

Among the harbingers of the New Age of Empowerment are the many young YouTube stars who have already figured out—many before they are teenagers—how to earn considerable incomes from doing what they love. They have realized early that by sharing their unique talents, (whatever they may be, from broad entertainment, to niche sharing, to instruction on game playing, flying and huge numbers of other things not taught in school) they can connect directly with their own world-wide "affinity group" that will support them and their work.

Reflection Question

Do you agree that we are moving to a New Age of Empowerment of young people? Why or why not? If so, it is good or bad? For whom?

Chapter 4

RE-FRAMING
WHO YOUNG PEOPLE ARE

From {Humans with Tools}
to [SYMBIOTIC EMPOWERED HYBRIDS]

NOW THAT WE HAVE re-framed the times in which young people live as the New Age of Empowerment, we can look to re-frame w*ho humans are in that Age*—re-framing both who young people have already become in many cases, and who they all are in the process of becoming. A dramatic increase in human capabilities is already underway, largely because of technology. It is therefore helpful to re-frame how we see the relationship of technology and humans.

Seeing Technology As a "Tool" is No Longer Helpful

The frame I most often hear for the relationship between humans and technology is that of *people with tools*. Most often these are seen as "optional" tools that humans can, with more difficulty perhaps, do without. "Tools are neutral," some also say. "They can be used for good or for bad." The problem is that one can say *exactly the same thing* about humans. So what?

I believe the frame of seeing technology as an optional, neutral tool is no longer helpful. In fact, framing "humans as the core" and "technology as an optional addition" is no longer even an accurate perspective. Already, in my view, and going forward, *technology has already become, and will continue to become a symbiotic part of 21st century humans.* It is already well down the road to becoming that today in many situations and places.

The re-frame we need is:

From technology as a tool, and humans in competition with it,

To humans becoming *SYMBIOTIC EMPOWERED HYBRIDS* with our technology.

Becoming symbiotic is hugely empowering.

Of course, humans are not the only species that uses tools. But as human "tools" progressed from sticks, to fire, to domestic animals, to extremely complicated machines—both helpful and destructive—they became more and more a part of us. How useful is a plumber without his tools? The use of tools enabled humans to extend and project our power far beyond our physical bodies and limitations.

But a big element of humans' frame for these tools, up until now is the idea that they are not part of humans' "essence." In that now-expiring frame, anything that has not biologically evolved "inside us" is just a "mere tool" that we have created and taught ourselves to use. Although these tools make us more powerful, they do not make us more human.

This is, essentially, a religious framing—of our relationship to "our maker" or to nature. In this frame, our body (including, of course, our brain)—along with, perhaps, some vaguely-defined spirit—completely comprises all of "who we are." At our core sits a "human essence"—which some connect directly with forces in the universe. Take away all our tools, and the human still remains.

Put Devices Down?

Ironically, as our technology becomes more and more powerful, we hear many adults asking young people (and in some cases all people) to put down their tools and shut off their technology—at least temporarily. I believe those asking for this do not yet realize that the old frame of humans with optional parts is changing—even biologically.

We now know a lot more about our biology, and particularly about the biome of microbes that lives in our gut and on our skin. All the bacteria in that biome—even the ones living in our gut—are actually *on the outside* of our blood-fed body, because we have a tube (the digestive system) running completely through us, and the bacteria are inside the tube. (This was a huge re-frame for me when I learned about it.) True, we didn't create the bacteria. But are they a "mere tool," created by nature? Or are they a part of us? Would it help us to "turn them off" from time to time? Doubtful. It would almost certainly lead to our demise.

I believe we will be better served, in our New Age of Empowerment, by revising the frame of "just a tool"—not only for the bacteria, but for technology as well. Were we to take away from modern humans every last vestige of 21st century technology they have today, including medical, dental, work tools, entertainment, and more, people, in most places, *would no longer be* 21st century humans—they would be "humans of the past." Some of these past human varieties still do exist in some places. While formerly we typically just wiped them out when we found them, we now go to great lengths to isolate and protect them and their way of life—both for their sake and as a kind of "museum" of our past. But although there will always exist a desire by some to live in earlier times, and although there will always be vestigial and atavist humans in corners of the modern world, most humans have already moved—or are quickly moving—to a new stage. We have been transformed by the environment we have created, and in which our young people will live.

Are we in Competition?

Some frame this new human stage—and Age—competitively. The 2011 book title *Race Against the Machine* [12] offers a frightening re-frame of the relationship of humans and technology as a competition between "humans" on the one side, and "technology" on the other. Although the authors' ideas are actually more nuanced than the title indicates, the frame of a war against technology has been adopted by not only authors and filmmakers, but by many parents as they see their kids become more and more attached to their smartphones. A great many adults are seriously frightened by today's young peoples' behavior regarding technology.

Symbiosis is a More Useful Re-frame

But that behavior doesn't need to be frightening. We can re-frame our new relationship with technology in a more useful, and hopeful way than us versus them—even though that makes for good movie plots. We can also do so in a way that is far more helpful than saying "We now have more advanced tools but they are still optional."

A far more useful re-framing is to view our relationship as *a new form of symbiosis*—producing a new kind of positive human-technology combination. I believe that to help our coming generations,

> **one of our greatest challenges is to make this symbiotic re-frame happen for them—and for all of us—as quickly and as completely as possible.**

Why Symbiosis?

What is this re-framing I am talking about? What *IS* symbiosis? And why is it so important for our children to frame their relationship to technology in this different way?

A "symbiotic relationship" is one in which two things need and depend on each other, because neither can survive (or survive as well) on its own. The combination is far more robust and powerful than either.

Humans today, I think many would agree, are less powerful without technology. And, certainly, technology is less powerful without humans to maintain and improve it. Neither would survive—at least in its current form—without the other.

That makes their relationship symbiotic. We each benefit from the other, and the whole is far better.

Young People Have Already Started

Young people, of course, have already begun moving to symbiosis just as fast as they possibly can. Almost everyone knows how hard it is to take away a young person's smartphone—parents try bribing and forcing their kids, teachers try oppressive rules. The young people get around both. *Why* is it so hard to take the technology away?

One theory is that the technology is addictive. I think, however, that that view, while common, is flawed. There *are* some things that the human body, once it experiences them, instantly craves—such as comfort. But we don't call people "addicted" to comfort. There are also powerful drugs, such as those anesthetists use. Trying these only once in the wrong way can lead to addiction in almost anyone. (It turns out a surprising percentage of anesthetists become addicted to the drugs they use. [13])

Technology, however, is useful to humans. Wanting more of it is a form of natural selection—those who have it thrive.

Some critics portray the idea of adults "maliciously" making technology addictive—i.e., by giving young people "dopamine hits" like rats in a cage to addict them to games or other technology. While doing this is certainly not outside of the lengths some adults will go for money or power, I believe a far better analogy for technology's worst effects are the negative effects gambling produces—it lures a small number to unhelpful behaviors, but not most.

That said, we should still pay attention, person-by-person.

A More Useful Frame

A far more useful re-frame for technology is to see it not as an addictive substance or behavior, *but more like humans having evolved a new body part.* People with the technology now have something that is *always with them* that serious extends their capabilities. It's very much like having a new limb, with new fingers that can reach out around the globe to places you want to be.

Because the technology—this new human body part—is so new, we have hardly mastered its use. One's real hand can be used both positively—to feed, caress, and pet—and also negatively—to punch, slap, and take what's not yours. But when young people do those undesirable things, parents and teachers don't cut young people's hands off. (Some once did, perhaps, but now that's

48

considered barbaric.) What they now do instead is they help the young people use their body parts more positively and productively. From the young people's point of view *it is barbaric* to take away their technology because they live in a new world—a world of symbiotic humans—where these things are a part of them.

For Whose Good?

Adults will claim, of course, they are taking the technology away "for the kids' own good." But what they usually mean is that it's for the good of the adults. It's the adults—and not the kids—who enjoy their dinner more when the kids are not staring at their phones. Often, what the adults are really trying to do is to keep an old culture going—i.e., to bring the kids back to the times and behaviors they (i.e., the adults) thought were better.

New Humans

But what if the young people don't think they are better? Smart phones didn't exist (in their current form) in the 20th century, when all adults grew up. Many of those same adults were told by their own parents to turn off their rock music. As far as we know, the rock music didn't do them any harm.

It didn't particularly help those young people either—it certainly didn't turn them into a new kind of human. But that is precisely what these new appendages are doing to our young people—turning them into a new kind of human—and in a very positive way. Today's young people can connect constantly to friends anywhere, to information they need, and to many forms of satisfaction. Already many kids now go most of their early life with ear buds and music, constantly in their ears. Their technology is becoming new parts of them, in a similar way to pacemakers, artificial heart valves or cochlear implants. Soon many more new technologies will move inside their bodies just as medical tools have already done. Screens, and even hand-held devices, will likely have been just an interim step to a more tightly-integrated symbiosis. What 21st century young person wouldn't want that?

Different things at Different Speeds

But it's not all happening at once. Look at this chart, and its three columns:

WE ARE MOVING FAST TOWARDS BECOMING 'SYMBIOTIC EMPOWERED HYBRIDS'

ALREADY SYMBIOTIC	ON THE WAY:	NOT YET SYMBIOTIC (but possibly coming)
	Debating	
Reading	Critical Thinking	LOVING
Writing (Non-fiction)	Project Management	DREAMING
Accessing Info	Systems Thinking	IMAGINING
Researching	Connecting Ideas	FEELING
Calculating	Writing (Fiction)	WARMTH
Translating	Art & Music	RESPECTING
Collaborating	Speaking	EMPATHIZING
Learning	Conversation	BEING ETHICAL
Agility	Relating	COMPASSION
Grit	Uniqueness	CREATIVITY
	ACCOMPLISHING	

Column 1: **"Already Symbiotic"**

The left-hand column consists of tasks where a great many of us are *already symbiotic* with technology. Although the means of the past still do exist to do the things in that column, few serious, 21st century people would do any of these things without incorporating technology in some form (if they have it)—just as very few would make a sign by carving it in stone. Some still do these things in the old way, but a growing number now read only on their smartphones, or through their ears, do all their research online, and use their calculator for everything arithmetical.

That is because *everything in the left-hand column can already be done faster and better by incorporating technology*—in many cases the technology already in your pocket (assuming, of course, the technology has reached you.) Despite being born in earlier times, I already do all the things in that column on my smartphone —and consider myself better off because of it. My 16-year-old son does even more. By the time they are adults, it is likely (and it should be our goal) that every young person born today in the world will have a connected device—today's smartphone or a better equivalent— with which to do these things.

Note that even for q "grit" or "stick-to-it-iveness"—qualities much sought after by parents—we are often much better off assigning our technology parts of the task to do (and using it to remind us to do our own parts) than trying to do it all ourselves. The machine parts never forget, get tired, or get bored—as humans often do.

Column 2: **"Well on Their Way"**

In addition to those listed in the first column, symbiosis is fast becoming the norm for a great many more human tasks—such as those in the middle column. Everything in that column is fast approaching a symbiotic state—i.e., the point at which doing them with technology is so much more powerful than without it that it makes little sense not to. For debating, check out IBM's *Project Debater* on You Tube (https://youtu.be/3_yy0dnIc58). It shows a Watson computer constructing and presenting an entire formal debate side, including opening statement, rebuttals, and conclusions. The computer, by itself, almost wins. In symbiosis with a human, it is the very best way.

I would particularly call your attention to art and music in this middle list. I personally got to watch the earliest beginnings of this still birthing symbiosis between art and technology as many guitar players—including Bob Dylan—switched from acoustic to primarily electric instruments. Today a great many young artists and musicians are in the process of becoming one with their new technology tools—moving far beyond the musical instrument and media tools of the past. There are now a great many interactive music and art performances and exhibitions where the technology lets the audience participate directly in the creative process—new kinds of art for the New Age of Empowerment.

Consider also "relating" and "accomplishing." Some young people already hone their conversation skills, in multiple languages, with A.I. chatbots like Siri. Old people in Japan and other places are using robots for companionship. People who are shy and/or autistic, often communicate more easily and comfortably through technology. In um, it is becoming harder and harder to accomplish *anything* new and different in the world without the use of some sort of technology. It helps us; we help it. That is called "symbiosis."

Column 3: **Coming Faster than We Think**

The activities in the right-hand column are often considered to be deeply "human." Many will opine that technology has not yet made many inroads there, and some would say it never will.

But that is not entirely true.

Although technology doesn't yet give us hugs and kisses, we can already have warm, loving conversations at a distance using technologies like Zoom, or even the telephone. (We could do this for a long while with writing, but not in real time.) I believe technology now allows humans to maintain *more* and *far better* warm and loving relationships at long distances. In our young people's lifetimes, technology will almost certainly be available to help us be more compassionate, empathetic, and even, I believe, ethical (for example, by monitoring our behavior and offering suggestions.)

So, while we may think of these "third column" things as more human and less symbiotic for the moment, that moment is unlikely to last long. Everything on the chart will, I predict, soon involve technology, in some symbiotically integrated way, for many or most people. I highly recommend you, the reader, start re-framing yourself and your children as "Symbiotic Human Hybrids."

Harbingers

Harbingers of the coming of Symbiotic Empowered Hybrids include every young person with a mobile phone who refuses to part with it just because an adult tells them they should. More advanced harbingers are the thousands of young people around the world who already have created real, world-improving, projects using technology symbiosis, such as the 15-year-old boy who invented a sandal for women in rural India to wear that captures the energy of her steps and gives her a loud alarm to sound if she is attacked, or the 13 year-old girl who created and app that identifies loved ones for Alzheimer's patients.

Reflection Question

Can YOU see young people in this new, "hybrid" way? What do you think are the implications?

Chapter 5

RE-FRAMING WHERE YOUNG PEOPLE WILL LIVE

From {on Earth and in their Imagination}
to [In their Imagination, on Earth & in the Cloud]

FOR MOST OF HUMAN HISTORY there were only two worlds that young people—and all people—could live in. One, of course, was the actual world—Earth—where everybody did physically live. Most lived their Earth lives in, or close to, the place where they were born—although automobiles and planes changed this a bit, in the 20th century. Dramatically changing locations in the Earth world was—and often still is—seen as adventurous and risky. Humans—analogizing themselves to plants—talk about putting down roots—i.e., connections to a physical community. Some, like refugees, are forced to move by circumstances, but few uproot themselves willingly. Many of those who leave their place of birth long to return—and often do. People tend to be tied to certain places on Earth, often, like salmon, to the place where they began.

Many see this as good. But it was, and still today is, a big limitation—especially for people whose place of birth (over which they had no control) happens to be less fortunate.

The World of Imagination

Yet no matter where they were located physically, humans have always had, as well, a second world to live in—the world of the imagination. Every human could—and most probably did—live some of the time inside their own imagined world. For many, that imaginary world made the physical world more palatable. Some chose to live there more than others. Those people who lived *mostly* in the world of their imagination were often seen by others as odd—artists at best, dreamers, pollyannas, or "crazies" at worst. But it is worth remembering that every human-made thing on Earth started in someone's imaginary world.

The Coming of the Cloud

Today we all—and especially young people—have a third world we can live in: "the Cloud." Although its origins go back to the mid-20th century, the Cloud didn't really exist as a place to live until the start of the 21st. Historically, the Cloud's birth time will be seen, almost certainly (in Western counting terms) as the turn of the second millennium.

The Cloud world is still rapidly evolving, both physically and in people's minds. Barring catastrophe, it will no doubt continue to evolve as long as there are humans. Humans will almost certainly create other places to live as well, such as on other planets. But it already clear that the Cloud is a new, different—and sometimes better—place to live for some—especially for many of the people born after the year 2000.

Science fiction writers have long imagined the Cloud's existence, and tried to describe it—the Oasis of *Ready Player One* is but one recent example. Once the Internet came not being people started building virtual worlds like Second Life online long before the current technology was fast enough for mass use. Now, with bandwidth growing rapidly, the technology is quickly catching up and the Cloud is burgeoning as an alternative place to exist.

What *IS* "the Cloud"?

The Cloud's definition is continually evolving; it changes almost from day to day. Currently, the Cloud is, in its physical being, millions of connected computers—called servers—mainly located in huge data storage facilities all over the globe. Symbiotically, with each other and with humans, these machines collectively create a new kind of reality—in software, rather than in physical space, often visible, and visitable, on screens or through VR goggles.

People access this new Cloud world—i.e., the software—though connections to the server network—sometimes through wires and cables but increasingly through the air. Humans interact with the Cloud in many ways—through the Internet and its World Wide Web, and through other programs, apps, screens, earbuds, and virtual reality headsets (among others). It is a world that is found not on Earth (other than in the growing number of server farms), but exists only in software—i.e., on humans' new symbiotic machine parts. But it is a world that is real—in a new way—and not just a metaphor.

Although it may evolve into something quite different, one can today picture the Cloud as an additional layer constantly receiving and beaming information, as in the artist's depiction in the figure below on the right of Elon Musk's Starlink satellites surrounding the planet.

Earth and Cloud will be Equal

Just like the Earth world, the Cloud is continually being fed by human investment and imagination.

How Should We "Frame" The Cloud?

The Cloud world is now extremely complex and deep and is daily becoming more so. Because it has become so much more complicated over its short existence, it requires some re-frames of its own.

The first is to the Cloud's being a "valid" reality:

From The Cloud being only a fantasy or gaming place—often dystopian (which it once may have been),

To the Cloud being as real, and important for people born in the 21ˢᵗ century, as life on Earth.

Instantiating Ideas

All man-made things existing in the Earth world began, as we noted, as an idea in someone's imagination. In that physical world, however, instantiating those ideas—i.e., bringing them into existence in the—was, and still often is, difficult. To get big things done it takes a great deal of physical resources. It is useful to also frame the Cloud a space for instantiation, i.e., for bringing ideas to reality:

> *The Cloud is a place where things that existed before only in the world of our imagination can get instantiated in new ways.*

In some cases—such as building a city, perhaps, or a monument—instantiating something in the Cloud is much less difficult than getting it built on Earth. Yet the Cloud also requires resources, sometimes a great deal of them. Those needed resources include computing power and, equally important, human brain power. But, in the Cloud world, many more of those resources can be centralized and, because they are software, more easily shared. (They are also more easily taken. A whole new debate has arisen around the ownership of intellectual property.)

The Cloud and Empowerment

Today, young people are discovering they are empowered to do all kinds of things in the Cloud world—including building lucrative businesses—all without leaving their homes and screens. Many of these are things that they previously couldn't do at all, or could do only with great difficulty. Rather than get a physical job—which he is not legally old enough, in many cases, to do—my 16-year-old son continually searches the Cloud and finds ways to earn money (legal ways, I hope.) The Cloud has already created many teenage millionaires. It has allowed me to conduct my own worldwide business (both writing and public speaking) entirely from my easy chair—something that at my now-advancing age, I very much appreciate.

The Comparative World Re-frame

The most useful perspective in the Age of Empowerment, I believe, is that neither the Earth world not the Cloud world is better than the other, or even more real. Both are places where human imagination can be brought to life in various ways.

So the useful re-frame needed is:

> *From On Earth / In Real-life always being better,*
>
> **To The Earth World and the Cloud World being equal.**

Hard to Accept?

Some adults find this "equal" re-frame hard to accept—it goes against much of what they have observed and thought. Many adults are today wary of young people (or even themselves) spending what they see as too much time in the Cloud and online. The online world is often thought of as dangerous.

But young people have already almost universally adopted this equal re-frame. Unless one does adopt it, a larger re-frame to the Age of Empowerment makes little sense, because the Cloud is one of its most empowering features.

Access Empowers

In fact, it is to a great extent the arrival of the Cloud that *makes* this the New Age of Empowerment. In my view, adults should make it a number one priority to see that every young person can access this new world at minimal or no cost—just as all should have access to food, water, and shelter on Earth. The arrival of the Cloud makes it far more imperative that nations that are currently behind in terms of getting fast Internet connection to all at affordable cost catch up.

Using our "new-part-of-the body" re-frame for technology, we can think of access to the Cloud access as a new **AORTA** (= **A**lways-**O**n **R**eal-**T**ime **A**ccess) [14] and make the following empowering re-frame:

> From 21st century humans being able to thrive in an old, unconnected way,
>
> **To a fast, reliable Cloud connection—i.e., a new AORTA** (Always-On Real-Time Access) **being now *required* to support newly-empowered human life.**

Having this new AORTA means a connected young person is now freed from Earth constraints and empowered in many new ways. They no longer require the same physical resources as in the past for getting things done, they can easily visit and explore faraway places and things, they are no longer prevented from interacting with people outside their local community, and are far less limited in realizing their imagination and dreams. Once a person is connected, the resources necessary to work in the Cloud—devices, software, knowledge, and connections—may be in many cases far more easily obtained (and shared) than the resources needed in the physical world.

It is interesting to see just how fast certain software capabilities are spreading among young people—often through just taking them, because they can, (what adults call "piracy") rather than through waiting until they had grown up and earned enough money to buy them. Being able to use resources that others have kept locked up is a form of empowerment—but one that goes against many old social rules and norms.

Harbingers

The harbingers of the new Cloud-is-equal world are the young people who have already flocked there in huge numbers. These cloud-based worlds appeared first in games, where they were populated mostly by the young. But they have expanded to all ages through Second Life, Verbela, Cloud-based live online schools, Cloud-based sales platforms (etsy), and Cloud-based competitive sports (including videogaming, trivia and chess) and betting. Much that was physical is being quickly duplicated in the Cloud, often *replacing* the physical. The Covid-19 pandemic accelerated the move to the Cloud world. Soon, I predict, there will be more conferences held in the Cloud than there will be in-person.

Reflection Question

How many worlds will your children live in? Will those worlds be accessible by all? Are adult's fears of these new worlds unfounded? Are we stopping them from getting there faster?

It's Not *Just* the Cloud that Empowers

As important as high-speed connection to the Cloud is to empowerment, the Cloud is not the only thing—or even the main thing—that is empowering young people in the 21st century. It is also young people's *changing beliefs*—largely about their role and what they can accomplish in this new Age of Empowerment—that is empowering them—as we shall now see.

Chapter 6

RE-FRAMING
WHAT YOUNG PEOPLE
BELIEVE

From {Unempowering 20th Century Beliefs}
to [Empowering 21st Century Beliefs]

THE NEXT STEP on our journey is for us to re-frame our understanding of *what young people are coming to believe.* This is crucial, because today beliefs are changing—quickly and globally—generationally.

In more and more instances and places, young people no longer believe what their parents did (or do) about many areas of life. Today's young people's deep, inner perspectives about more and more things are often very different from those of the adults that preceded them, and often their own parents. This became very clear to me when I spoke at a school in Abu Dhabi. All the young people—still traditionally neatly dressed in white thoubs and black niqabs—literally pleaded with me to speak "not to us, but to our parents"—because the differences in beliefs were so great. Those young people are not alone.

So let us examine "beliefs" more carefully.

What Are Beliefs?

Everyone has beliefs.

I call them our frames. Others call them our mindsets, or worldviews. They are among humans' most fundamental and personal thoughts—the deepest ways we choose to see, and interpret, the world. They typically form when we are young, and are selectively and continuously reinforced throughout most of our lives—particularly our early lives. One important result of this continuous, selective reinforcement is that we often view our own, personal beliefs as "truths."

It is therefore often quite a shock when we come up against others with different—particularly opposing—beliefs. It often leads to fighting, and even to war. It can be *even more* of a shock when, as adults, we see beliefs that we hold deeply and dearly changing significantly in our children—despite our most strenuous attempts to instill our beliefs into them through parenting, schooling, patriotism and/or religion.

Generational Belief is What's Happening

But "generational belief change" *IS* what is taking place now. It is happening in a big way, and to a much greater extent than it has in the past. It requires a big re-frame on many people's part:

> *From our own beliefs being truths forever,*
>
> **To beliefs, in many cases, changing to fit the times.**

An important implication of this new change in frame is that, to move forward,

> *It is the adults, not the young people, who must now change their beliefs to fit the changing times.*

This is not an easy thing for many adults to accept, or to do. As I write in 2021, all adults were born in the 20th century. Wherever they grew up, it was in a 20th century context that all of their early beliefs were formed. Those beliefs were reinforced and confirmed by, in many cases, decades of 20th century adult experiences.

In a recent conversation I had with a well-known, well-respected business leader, he began a sentence to me with "All my experience tells me that..." Yet all his (20th century) experience didn't make him right in today's context—he was incorrect in his conclusion. In the new, 21st century environment, his, and many other adults' beliefs about how the world works—i.e., their frames—are completely wrong for what is coming.

Another big implication is that

> *We ALL need to re-examine our deeply-held and often unconscious beliefs—because a great many of today's adults' old 20th century beliefs no longer help in the 21st century.*

Not Just in One Area

Perhaps the most interesting thing to me is just how broad the generational change in beliefs is. Several years ago, working with Australian cultural anthropologist Genevieve Bell, I put together this list:

BELIEFS ARE CHANGING GENERATIONALLY
in many key areas of life...

Technology	**Security**	**Money**
Privacy	Power	**Love**
Property	Work and Jobs	**Violence / Abuse**
Personal	Empathy	Justice
Relationships	Kids	Government
Sexuality / Race	God and Religion	Time & Space

and more!

And here are some of the generational changes we now see:

AREA	OLD BELIEFS	NEW BELIEFS
Technology	Tools	Symbiosis
Privacy	Super important	Trade-offs
Property	Own your own	Share
Personal Relationships	Local / in-person	Global / Virtual OK
Sexuality / Race	Intolerant	More tolerant
Security	Unlikely	Possible
Power	Adults only	Shared
Work & Jobs	Not satisfying OK	Satisfaction required
Empathy	Little	Much more
Kids	Little us's, not yet capable	Unique, Capable
God & Religion	Very important/widespread	Less important/less widespread
Money	Earn and save, investment is for the rich	investment / crypto
Love	Local / Man & Woman	Anywhere / Many kinds
Violence/abuse	Tolerated	Not tolerated
Justice	For some	For all
Government	Useful	Questioned
Time & Space	Separators	No longer separators

I have not the space, in this volume, to explore each of these in more detail—I hope to do so in future writings. I do highly recommend, however, that you carefully go through each item on the list, asking yourself whether your own beliefs and those of the young people you know, coincide. And if they don't, reflecting on how do the beliefs of the young people differ from yours (and possibly why).

Re-framing Beliefs About Growing Up: The Beliefs Divide

In the chart below, I resume how I think beliefs are changing in the particular area that concerns us here: that of young people growing up in the 21st century. It is yet another way to re-frame what I see as a growing *beliefs divide* between the generations:

20th c. BELIEFS: (Disempowering)	The Emerging BELIEFS DIVIDE	21st c. BELIEFS: (Empowering)
- Kids can't accomplish much		- Empowered Kids can make an impact
- Learning comes first		- Accomplishing comes first
- Technology is just a "tool"		- Technology is a symbiotic part of us
- In-person is always better		- Earth & Cloud are equal
- Individual work comes first		- Teams & Collaboration come first
- Kids need knowledge & skills from adults		- Kids need empowerment & coaching from adults
- Education — as we do it — remains important and necessary		- Preparing for the future is needed; but 20c. education NOT the best way

We see in the chart a stark differentiation between old 20th century beliefs and new 21st century beliefs regarding young people. How much do you think this beliefs divide affects our young people as they grow up? My sense is quite a bit. By encouraging or forcing our old beliefs on our young people, I believe we seriously hold them back from where they could and should be going. As indicated by the labels, most of the old 20th century beliefs about young people are *dis*empowering and need to be rethought for the Empowerment Age.

66

Thus another, suggested re-frame:

> *Your beliefs may have been quite useful for the times in which you grew up,*
>
> **But forcing your old beliefs on young people—no matter how near and dear those beliefs may be to you—is unhelpful to them.**

Beliefs and Empowerment

Some beliefs are more empowering than others. It is possible for both adults and young people to hold beliefs that are disempowering—or empowering—for young people. The big shift I see happening is to more empowering beliefs being held by young people. This—along with new technologies—are what is driving those young people into the new Age of Empowerment.

Disempowering Beliefs

The beliefs on the left of the above chart—in particular the old beliefs -that kids can't accomplish much while they are young, -that years of learning must come first, -that technology is just an optional "tool" often better put aside, -that in-person is always better than remote or virtual, -that kids require all the past knowledge we can put into them, -that collaboration is cheating, and -that education as we do it is absolutely necessary for a person's advancement in the world—are all extremely disempowering for today's young people.

Empowering Beliefs

On the other hand, the set of new beliefs on the right -that young people can accomplish with impact, -that accomplishment comes before (and is the motivation for) learning, -that technology is a symbiotic part of us, -that the Earth world and the Cloud world are equal, -that young people need empowerment and coaching from adults rather than information, -that teamwork and collaboration are crucial in their times, and -that education and school (as the world delivers those things) are not be the best preparation for the future—are all enormously empowering.

I recommend asking yourself:

> **How many of the *empowering* 21st century beliefs**
> (on the right of the chart) **do I agree with and hold?**
>
> **Do my own beliefs need reframing for the 21st century?**

Harbingers

My favorite proponent of the change to empowering beliefs is Kiran bir Sethi, from Ahmadabad, India. In 2011 she decided her own children—and all children—needed a change to an "I can" belief, rather than just academic success. She founded a school (the Riverside School in Ahmadabad) out of which grew *Design for Change (DFC)*, an organization which is now in over 60 countries. That organization has empowered hundreds of thousands of kids all over the world, by enabling them to them accomplish tens of thousands of projects with Measurable Positive Impact on their communities. In 2018 Pope Francis hosted over 3,000 of these young people from around the world in Rome and at the Vatican, where they shared their projects with each other and the world. (http://dfcworld.com.)

Reflection Questions

Do you see beliefs changing in young people? In what areas? What are some old beliefs that you hold onto most dearly? Do you think any of them will be less useful to the people in our coming world?

And now, with some idea in mind of what young people are coming to believe, let us look at their future world, and their aspirations for that world. These are also in serious need of re-framing.

Chapter 7

RE-FRAMING OUR YOUNG PEOPLE'S FUTURE WORLD

From {a World of Experience}
to [a New Frontier for Exploration]

WHAT IS THE MOST USEFUL WAY TO RE-FRAME THE FUTURE as we enter the new Age of Empowerment? I suggest it is most useful to frame it as a "new frontier," where humans have never been before. On this new frontier, our young people are moving from "a world of experience" to "a world of exploration."

The Old World of Experience

Our old world was run, almost entirely, on experience. Useful things typically lasted a long time and became "tried and true." Changes, when they arrived, came very gradually. Most things, and situations, had been seen before, in some form, by previous generation(s).

In that world, knowing about those seen-before things was what counted most—it was what produced so-called wisdom. In that before-now world, the more experience you had, the wiser you were. Age, with its lived experience, always trumped youth, which lacked it. Experience in the world, combined with knowledge of the past, was one of the most helpful things one could have. It was why we studied history. It was why many places venerated old people. Experience mattered.

Part of that frame—and world—was that the future, for young people, came slowly and gradually. Most things continued throughout one's lifetime very much as they were, changing, at most, only incrementally. Some things didn't change at all (many, in the old frame, thought that included "human nature.") Moreover, the world often seemed to work in cycles, returning to things, and conditions seen before.

The Value of Experience is Changing

That old frame of experience being so valuable is now less and less useful. As the world changes, *experience is good only for maintaining the old world.*

A far more useful re-frame for our young people's future is this:

From a world where experience counts most,

To a world where exploration is key.

"The Frontier" as a Better Frame

The concept of the frontier has long been with us—as a reality, a myth, and a metaphor. It occurs and re-occurs over history as humans move from place to place and continent to continent—and it exists in our imaginations as well. Some may remember, as I do, "The New Frontier" being U.S. President John F. Kennedy's campaign slogan in the 1960's.

The frontier metaphor can be inspiring—Kennedy's use of it inspired humans to get to the moon. Today, as we now approach a new frontier of space beyond the moon, we are also at a new frontier here on Earth—**a world that is changing.** Yet to many, that new frontier on Earth is less inspiring—and more fear-inducing. But the only humans who have to fear are those afraid of change. Those are quite a few in number, but, thankfully, not all.

Expanding the Metaphor

To more helpfully understand and re-frame the new frontier to which humanity has arrived, let me expand the metaphor as a story, or movie script:

IMAGINE, if you will, our young people's future world as a newly discovered place. (You can use America or Australia for Europeans in the 1600's as your metaphorical model if it helps.)

Now imagine people in the old world—the only world they know—slowly beginning to hear of this new one and realize it exists, although only its vaguest outlines are known and can be seen on some maps.

Some intrepid pioneers actually make the journey, get there, and survive. They build up colonies on the coastline and send word back. Gradually, others follow.

As more and more arrive and multiply, the coastline quicky gets crowded, with far less room for each of the people there than there was at first. Many of the new inhabitants—especially the young people born there, now trying to find their place in this new world—start to feel constrained.

The Scary Forest

Just a little way in from the coast, on this imaginary new continent, is a huge, dark, extremely dense forest. Pretty much every adult living on the coast regards the forest as a very, very scary place. Some occasionally venture in—mostly just a bit at the edges. A very tiny few do some deeper exploration of the forest, and built some things for their own use while there.

Most of the adults on the coast don't want, or permit, their children to go into the forest at all. "Maybe later," the adults tell them—"when you have grown up." The young people know that if they grow up like their parents did, they will likely never go in either.

So the young people do go in on their own—lots of them, deeper and deeper, mostly when their parents aren't watching. A few return with scars, increasing the adults' belief that the woods are incredibly dangerous.

Still, more and more young people are anxious to go there. For one thing, the crowded coast is no longer a place they want to be, particularly with all the adults fighting for space. They see many of the things on the coast—things they were brought up to look forward to—disappearing or growing old.

Wonderful Things

Plus the young people report—mainly to each other, through their own channels—finding wonderful new things in the woods. They climb the forest's tall trees (often with the help of devices that the first explorers built and left), and in the treetops they discover a new world, where they can play and communicate in new, exciting ways.

The young people almost all love doing this. They enjoy living in this new world that didn't exist before, and many thrive there. It is not clear yet what is best to do there, so they try out a variety of activities—some of them new versions of what was left to them by old people, but mainly things newly-invented by them. Occasionally, in trying these things, they fall out of the trees and get hurt, but the young people still really want to be there. They see it as a new, less-constraining environment, where they have much more opportunity and control over their lives than they do on the coast. It's a world that has many more places for them to go and be in—both in the trees and on the ground.

But even so, their parents *still* don't want them to be there. "Come back and live with us," they continue to plead.

Doing More

Gradually, the young people start to realize they can do more and more in the woods than their parents ever could do on the coast or back in the old country. They start building their own structures and their own lives and start letting go of and abandoning the ways of their parents. A new frontier mentality of "we are building things anew for our own use" sets in. They invent new rules for themselves.

They do know the woods have dangers—there are harmful predators and swamps that some fall into, with a few actually suffering and dying. But far more they see exciting opportunities. Relatively few get seriously hurt, and each time someone is hurt, they try to find ways to prevent it from happening again.

And...

Back on the coast, (as the young people increasingly enjoy their experiences in the woods), the ocean, unfortunately, begins gradually rising up—making the already-crowded coast a lot smaller and a lot less pleasant a place to be. The adults there are increasingly frightened of drowning, but they *still* don't want to go into the forest—so they try to cut the forest down. Sadly for them, they can't, because the forest (where most of their children now live) is becoming ever more robust, and goes on and on, seemingly forever. They flounder, looking for other solutions.

Meanwhile ...

Inside the forest, the young people are thriving in the new, exciting, dual world of ground *and* treetops they've entered. Some adults, seeing their warnings failing to keep the young people out, and worried about losing them, attempt a different approach. They send in their old ways from the coast relabeled as "medicine" and "care packages," including in shiny, new, modern-looking "reformed" schools and teachers. All of those come with urgent messages to the young people to "please come in, it's for your own good, this will help you succeed on your journey." But the kids reject these revised versions of the old world and prefer to find their own way through the forest. And they do.

Success for the kids, but...

Sadly, although there are individual tries here and there, most of the adults never put more than a toe into the forest, despite the growing realization that only way to survive is to go deeply into it and learn to climb the trees. Most of the adults continue to flounder on the ever-shrinking coast they know—and still love—until the sea finally takes them.

###

The moral is that it is better to re-frame the journey:

From sticking to the place where you are comfortable and keep your children with you —even as it goes away

To seeing where the young people are headed and letting them go there—despite your fears—because you recognize that the future, for them, is better there.

Note, by the way, that "Feeling the fear and doing it anyway" **is the** *definition* **of courage.**

Harbingers

A harbinger of the triumph of exploration over experience is Oliver Daemen, who went to space in 2021 as Blue Origin's first paying customer. Clearly fortunate to have a very wealthy father, the then 18-year-old Oliver was ats that time the youngest person to ever go to space. Previously, decades of experience were required to be an astronaut. But Oliver had not done that, because in the New Age, he didn't need to—he could explore space while still young.

20 years from now, going to space will likely be a normal component of many young teams' real-world projects. But there will always be new frontiers for young people to explore, and they will always go there being inexperienced.

Reflection Question

Where in our world do you see experience as already less valuable (and perhaps even constraining)?

Chapter 8

RE-FRAMING OUR YOUNG PEOPLE'S ASPIRATIONS

From {Becoming Generational Replacements}
To [Becoming Continual Inventors]

NOW THAT WE HAVE RE-FRAMED THE FUTURE as a new frontier of exploration, let us re-frame what young people should aspire grow up to become on that frontier. (Later, in Parts III and IV of the book, I re-frame the process that requires.)

Today, when an adult meets a young person—of almost any age—one of the first questions they often ask is "What do you want to be when you grow up?"

That is because we have lived, up through the 20th century, in a world of *replacement*. Our societies were very much like adult human bodies, in the sense that, while one is alive, the body continues with only gradual apparent change—while all its cells swap out, regularly and continuously, for new ones. All (or almost all) our individual body cells continually die and get replaced—some as frequently as every few days—and yet we appear the same person.

Societies can be seen as a set of roles, with individual people as cells filling those roles. Just as in our body, in society the cells (in this case the people) get replaced regularly—more or less every

77

generation. But the roles remain, and the society continues to look pretty much the same, except in small ways.

A Left-Over Frame from a Former World

In the replacement world we lived in through the 20th century, a big need was to prepare young people to become these replacement cells. Guiding their growing-up process was the way we did it.

And in the relatively slow-changing societies before now—in which younger people came to replace, gradually over decades, older people who retired or passed away—maintaining a relatively strict distinction between "adults" (who filled roles) and "replacement-adults-in-training" (children who will eventually fill the roles) may have been useful and made some sense. In the times when almost all the roles were pre-defined an adult, was not just someone older, but a person who had found a particular role to play *and* who had gotten the experience necessary to play it successfully. A child, in that world, was only a future replacement—someone who was still in the process of still deciding who (in a general sense) they wanted to replace and preparing for their eventual take-over of a role. A grown-up person who hadn't replaced any adult role was still considered a child—a Peter Pan.

Who Chooses?

The replacement choice for young people was often made by their parents, who sent them either into their own profession, or to apprenticeships, or to various kinds of vocational training (e.g., the priesthood, or medical school.) In some places and families children had more choice as to what their replacement role would be than in others. But few children, if any, did any actual adult roles while young (other than perhaps as a hereditary king or substitute parent,).

Raising kids, in cases where their future adult role was not pre-determined, often involved exposing them to various professions and role models that needed replacing to see which they were attracted to. Some of this was aspirational for parents, based on their own experiences and dreams. In some places it was considered helpful to provide young people with as many models as possible, so they could choose one they liked.

But even in those places, we didn't do a very good job. Not only did most young people see only a tiny fraction of all that is out there to choose from, but many "exposers" also tried hard to constrain them to the replacement choices they thought would be best for themselves or for their society—and not necessarily for the young people. Every generation needed new doctors, lawyers, engineers, and accountants, and, because the earnings from those professions were good, parents (and other adults) often pushed their children in those directions. Other adults paved the way for their children into whatever work they did themselves. Most tried to discourage young people from replacing low earning jobs.

Replacement Everywhere

Replacement is not necessarily a good strategy for empowering young people. But growing up, up until now, was almost entirely a process of generational replacement. Replacement is, today, the way almost everything works: companies, professions, family businesses (including farms), trades and crafts, as well as governments. New businesses (or newly forming countries) clone the existing roles from older ones and then fill and replace those. As societies expand, more people are often needed in some roles and fewer in others. Some roles may evolve or disappear, but new roles are only rarely created.

In a replacement world—i.e., our world up until now—the question "What do you want to be when you grow up?" really means *"Whom do you want to replace?"* There is only a single, overall role for any young person—adult replacement in training. That is why it scares many adults when someone says, "X percent of the jobs of the future have not been invented yet." How do they prepare young people for those jobs, when all we know is how to replace?

"Real Experience" Was What Truly Counted

In the slow-changing, replacement world before now, most things, in most jobs, *had been seen before* in some form. The precise situation could, of course, differ, and some things were seen only rarely. So to be a good replacement you needed to have seen as many of those things as possible. That meant you needed a lot of "real-world experience"—acquired mostly on-the-job while performing the actual role (or at least being an assistant.) In a "replacement" world the smart criterion for hiring someone was "Has he or she done this before successfully?" The most critical question for an adult hiring a replacement to ask in that world, was "How much relevant experience do you have?"

Experience meant real, lived circumstances—younger people didn't have it because they hadn't lived long enough.

For example, when I and my wife needed a pediatrician for our newly born son, our obstetrician strongly recommended that we choose an older, almost-retired doctor. "He may seem old," the recommender said, "but he's *seen everything.*" The newer replacement doctors—although certified MDs who had hopefully been shown the latest innovations in medical school, had little real-life experience and so, in his view, were not the best.

In the replacement world young people *weren't even considered* for most roles because they clearly lacked experience by virtue of their fewer years on the planet. The most effective hiring strategy was luring experienced people away from competitors—known as "poaching." Some training schools, such as Harvard Business School, tried to compensate through reading and discussing stories about others' experiences—what they called the "case method.

Re-Framing Experience

But more recently, two key things changed. The first was that we began developing and honing new ways, besides "time-in-grade," to get experience. Substitutes for actual experience—sometimes called "ersatz" (i.e., replacement) experience—could come not just through the case studies I mentioned, but through things like imaginary visualizations, and, increasingly, through computer-based simulations. I was once told, for example, that the U.S. military expects any person who wants to be a pilot to have mastered all the commercially available jet fighter programs on his or her own before they show up.

These new techniques increased the scope of previously-seen problems one could see in advance, and let trainees deal with them (with some feedback)—thus reducing, in some cases, the amount "lived experience" needed. With the spread and increasing power of computers in the early 21st century, simulation has spread to many more jobs and professions. One of the problems we are still struggling with in this form of non-lived experience is that the behavior of machines is far easier to predict and simulate than is the behavior of people. But even as we get better at this, something else is happening.

But Now Less Need

Far more importantly, as the world changes and innovation and invention increases, *lived experience itself—including with people—has started becoming less necessary and helpful.* In fact, lived experience—knowing how to do something well in the "old" world—might actually be a hindrance in the new.

Taken together, these two changes, made this re-frame of our young peoples' future needs a far more useful way to see the world:

> *From replacing someone in an existing adult role.*
>
> **To inventing new adult roles for oneself.**

Today, the re-framed question that adults should now be asking each young person they meet is:

> *"What new role do you want to invent for yourself and for the world?"*

When to Start?

Today, the time to start inventing these roles is not when one becomes an adult, but immediately. I have already mentioned the too oft-heard-from-adults dictum that "X percent of the jobs of the future have not been invented yet." For a young person today, it makes no sense to wait for them to be invented. They need to start inventing them themselves—based not on supposed future needs, but on who they uniquely are. This is new.

Before now, i.e., in the 20th century when today's adults grew up, relatively few employers—outside, perhaps, of R&D—hired employees based on their "expected invention." For one thing, invention was disruptive. But today "disruption" and "innovation" are what employers are (or should be) looking for.

"Non-lived" Experience

And even in those cases where we think experience is still helpful, we are moving quickly, as we have seen, to "non-lived" experience. It is worth remembering that we have always had such non-lived experience—that is precisely what stories are—told, read, or viewed. It is why the case method worked. Now new—and often far better— forms of non-lived experience are becoming available in the Cloud, and they can come from people both real and virtual.

The simulations I mentioned are not the only way to get non-lived experience—with the Cloud there are many more. I often ask young people what You Tubes they watch—the answer reveals not just their interests, but also much of their virtual experience. We now, with virtual reality, have real-world "telexperiences" young people can get and use, such as actually doing part of a live medical operation. Even "imagined experience" such as the visualizations that coaches use, helpfully, with athletes, can provide virtual experience online. Stories and classes—although still useful—need to be re-framed as *old-fashioned ways* for a young person to prepare for (someday) replacing someone in a role, when that is the goal, there are now, and will soon be, many other—and often better— ways.

We need a re-frame

> *From living and reading as the best forms of experience,*
>
> **To many new forms of experience.**

Replacing Experience with Invention

Yet even as it becomes easier and easier to *get* new forms of useful experience for replacement tasks, **replacement is less and less what we need**. Our young people are entering a world where whatever roles they are desirous of one day replacing may very well be gone by the time they grow up. This includes manual workers, intellectual roles (such as doctors), and, in fact, *every role that exists in multiple instances in different places, i.e., where the person (such as post office workers) does almost exactly the same thing in each place.* All those roles will be automated in our young people's future. Post offices already have automated clerks, and we are very close to the point where almost anything that can be done equally well by more than one person can be done by a machine.

So it is time to re-framing our young peoples' aspirations

> *From getting as much "relevant" experience as possible,*
>
> **To inventing new roles for themselves, in function of their unique dreams, interests, talents and passions.**

In the past most organizations—whether companies, sports teams, or governments—were always seeking replacements. Whole professions—headhunters, sports/talent scouts, political recruiters—arose for finding people with the "right" experience and potential. As the stakes got higher, fewer employers took chances. The key hiring criteria became only "relevant experience" and "fit." Individuals with radically new and different ideas only rarely had a chance. Any new ideas were introduced only gradually, if at all.

Now, going forward, this has changed dramatically. What was rarely desired in the replacement world—invention and innovation—is precisely what is needed in more and more roles— and soon, in all.

From a Few to Everyone

Some roles, of course, were always about invention. They were typically the most complex roles—from running a country, to waging a war, to running a large company (or even a startup, few of which succeed.) Because there were too many variables involved in these roles—especially the people—there was no "right way" to do any of them. I naively expected, when I went to Harvard Business School almost 50 years ago, having previously been a musician—a profession where there is generally a right way to play an instrument (although not to interpret music)— that they would teach me "how to do business." What I discovered, to my surprise, is that *no one knew*—the people at the top just made it up as they went along. That was why Harvard used the case method of reading lots of stories about difficult situations and trying to imagine what we would do. What they were really trying to teach was "how to invent on the fly."

Now, in the new age of Empowerment, that invent-on-the-fly process needs to be absorbed by everyone. The decision of whether to choose "an experienced person" for every role (like the pediatrician who has seen everything)—or to choose someone who is inexperienced but innovative, is being re-made everywhere, at every level.

"Role Model" thus takes on a very different meaning. What we ask our young people need to be re-framed:

> *From "Whom do you want to be like, or replace when you grow up?"*
>
> **To**
> - What are your dreams?
> - What do you think you can become?
> - What do you want you invent?
> - What, that is new, do you want to accomplish?

For those who grew up in the far-simpler replacement world, this can be very scary.

Harbingers

Harbingers of young people choosing to be inventors rather than replacements include all the young people who opted to create new careers in the Cloud as it grew. This included inventing new roles such as "search engine optimizer" and "You Tube channel creator and personality." Many young people got wealthy inventing these roles. Many companies, in order to find people who could do this, began adding "digital native" to their job requirements—used as a thinly veiled euphemism for "young".

Reflection Question

Will you change the questions you now ask young people you meet? Or the questions you ask to the people you plan to hire? What new questions will you ask? What new non-replacement roles have you seen?

Chapter 9

RE-FRAMING
WHAT'S UNIVERSAL FOR
ALL YOUNG PEOPLE

From {Academic Success}
to [Accomplishing with Impact]

THE SPREAD OF 20ʰ CENTURY EDUCATION—which
for most people means school and academics—was an extremely
important feature of the time. It was only in the last century that the
idea of bringing education to all young people finally spread around
the globe. And it was only in the 20th century that a frame of getting
at least some formal academic education and schooling came to be
seen as a "universal" need for young humans. This frame culminated
in the United Nations' designating, in 2015, "quality education for
all" to be its Fourth Sustainable Development Goal (SDG 4) for the
2015-2030 period.

But by the time the United Nations got to creating this goal, it
was already time to re-frame it, because the world had moved
forward.

Is Formal Academic Education a Universal Need?

Having a formal education was extremely useful in the 20th century. What a formal education meant—throughout the world—was some kind of academic schooling, with teachers who taught a standard curriculum to young people in classrooms. (The very rich had tutors, one-on-one.) Because the benefits of formal education were often very clear to those who went through it, there was a strong desire to extend it to all—and to make it a "quality" education (usually defined as a rigorous academic program with dedicated teachers and high standards) as well. As the SDG says, humans' 20th century goal is "universal high-quality academic education for all."

But is "universal academic education for all"—even with quality— a useful goal for the 21st century? Is it, in fact, a goal that we should have for all young people in the future? Asked differently, *is some form of academic education something every young human can, and should, usefully do?*

Today, at the start of the 21st century, certainly, a great many still think so. But I disagree.

Re-framing What is Universal

I believe that, in the new Age of Empowerment, this perspective requires a re-frame. It turns out "having academic success" is *not* something universal to all. A great many try and fail. So what *is* universal?

> **What *is* universal to every human—something every human young or old is capable of—is "setting a positive goal for themselves (at some level) and accomplishing it with impact."**

That, as we have defined it, is *EMPOWERMENT*.

So the re-frame of "what's universal" for young people is:

From every young person needing and getting an academic education,

To every person becoming empowered through accomplishing with positive impact.

Why an Academic Education is NOT a Universal Need

"Academic education," which many love, is a tradition that started relatively late in human existence. A tiny number experienced its beginnings a few millennia ago, in ancient Greece and other places. But for a very long time after its conception, formal academic education was restricted, very deliberately, to only a very few individuals in the world.

It is only in recent centuries that certain skills—particularly reading, writing and arithmetic, became seen, in places as useful for all to have. Formal academic education was mandated by Prussia in the 18th century, then by much of Europe. Standard academic curricula were established at the end of the 19th century in the U.K., and in the U.S. But much of the world didn't have such criteria at all. Even by the mid-20th century, academic education was far from universal. Only a tiny fraction of all the young people in the world (probably less than 5 percent) attended university. In many places young people did not even attend primary school.

That is now seen, by many, as a societal great failing which we need in the 21st century to correct.

But do we? Or do we need to move on?

The 20th Century Population Explosion

In the century between the years 1920 and 2020 the world's human population quadrupled. Today, in 2021, there are more *young people* in the world than there were *people* in the world 100 years ago. (1920 total world population: 1.9 billion; 2021 under 25 population: 2-3 billion.)

As these 2-3 billion young people grow up in our new world of great diversity and uniqueness, as well as automation and AI, we need to re-ask the question: ***"What can (and should) <u>every one</u> of them be doing as they grow up?"***

Put slightly differently, that question is

What is universal to all young people—that we can, and should, encourage for their future development?

In the 20th century we thought we had found that answer. It was: "being educated, in the academic way."

But that turned out to be wrong. The academic education solution worked only for some, and it worked only in the context of the 20th century. Now we must get it right for our young people's future—not least because there are now so many of them!

It's *NOT* Academic Education, As We Thought

In the 20th century academic education brought a great many people to a new and better place—including many of the readers of this book. Unfortunately, however, academic education's effects were not universal. Some took to it, and benefitted from formal, academic education—but many did not. A great many people—

probably the vast majority of people in the world—do not fit the narrow, constricting "academic mold" originally designed for only a tiny sliver of the population. Academic education does not work universally because not everybody wants to—or can— meet its particular demands. The behaviors it requires are today far too restrictive for most young people in the world. Many who start down that path fail and dropped out. And almost everyone who *does* get through it in the end, has to be "pushed" through much of it—in many cases pushed hard—by educators and parents. That is not a particularly good sign.

What we got from all these efforts was social mobility and a better life for some, and possibly some better prepared workers for our factories. But we are very far from that having been true for all.

So, as good a solution as academic education may have been *for its times*, those times have now passed. Although formal academic education, as we created it and set it up all around the world, benefitted a great many—and although it made great impacts in the 20th century all over the globe, it never—despite heroic efforts—reached, or helped, everybody. Sadly, education, as it was conceived and implemented in the 20th century, is NOT—and cannot be—universal, as we once hoped. Why not? I can think of at least three main reasons:

Reason 1: It's Too "Academic"

The first reason that it is not a universal solution is that formal education, as it evolved into and through the 20th century, became almost entirely "academic," i.e., about nomenclature, a limited set of skills, especially literacy and numeracy, and thinking in specific structured ways. That more tightly structured approach almost completely replaced the ad-hoc parent-to-child and apprenticeship methods from before. Academic education lays out a single path to success, very well-known to most today. It is "Show up consistently and on time, get good grades, finish as high in your class as you can, get your degree (ideally from a place with a high reputation), and then go on for as many more degrees as you can." Knowing and following that pattern today gets you a job, pretty much anywhere.

But not everyone can, or wants to, do that.

Not everyone, it turns out, is cut out for academics. As we pushed more and more people into school, the non-succeeders became labelled as failures and were de-valued. After, perhaps, some additional trying, we either gave them something lesser to do (e.g., vocational education) or let them drop out and fend for themselves. For those who stayed we established numerous hierarchies based on degrees of academic success, and created and required gateways (such as the SAT, college rankings and admissions committees) to measure a person's success and allow them entry into those hierarchies. In many places, we even made academic success synonymous with being a good, successful young person.

But in doing this, we gave every person who failed to follow the pattern successfully a big handicap in society. So we tried harder extended the system—spending huge amounts of time, treasure, and effort trying to push *all* of our young people into getting as much academic education as possible. Even as it became clear that only some of them wanted it, or would benefit from it, we still wanted it. 20th century adults considered academic education crucial for all.

Failure at Something That Everyone Considers Crucial is *Harmful*

The reality, however, is that most people in the world are NOT big academic successes. The frame that academic education is crucial for success in the world turns out to be extremely *harmful* to many of our young people. We very often forget—or ignore— that

> **Those who do not thrive on academics are *not only* equal to the others in other respects, but they are also far more numerous.**

Another Reason Academic Education is NOT a Universal Need

A second reason that education is NOT the universal need and solution we thought it was, is that the human population is now much larger, and more diverse. As we noted, the world population exploded five-fold between 1900 and today. (1.6 billion in 1900; 7.8 billion in 2021.) It is fair to say, I think, that—although their parents may want it for them—most of these newly added people are not interested in "academic education" per se. What they are interested in, rather, is *realizing their dreams and goals.*

What has changed is that the best means to that goal, for most, is not academic education but *real-world accomplishment.* (Academic education can and does still work for some, of course, but only for a relative few, and only very indirectly.)

The Third Reason

The third reason that academic education is no longer the universal solution it was thought to be is *the arrival of the Digital Age*—which started roughly around the year 2000. This has produced, and is still producing, a generation of people who (1) are acquiring many new capabilities on their own, through the spread of technology, (2) have new and different beliefs, and attitudes, and (3) are unwilling to accept the terms and constraints that an academic education comes with.

Technology: A Great Boon for Humanity—but a False Hope for Academic Education

An initial belief of many from the 20th century—particularly in Silicon Valley—was that digital technology would enable us to do academic education not only more widely, but also better. But that has turned out, despite huge investments, not to be true.

The technology advocates are *not* wrong about technology's power to spread, but they are on the wrong track about what it can do well. it turns out that technology does not provide huge improvements to academic education—or even much support for it, other than with different access, fancier graphics, better record-keeping, and, often, meaningless statistics. But,

---

What technology DOES support—and support greatly— is EMPOWERMENT.

Academic Education is Becoming an Artifact

Although few are willing to, or want to admit it, academic education is no longer on the ascendency in the world. Although it will probably last, as a niche, forever academic education has begun an inevitable decline—despite heroic efforts to revive and spread it—because it is no longer needed in the same way.

Here is another re-frame:

> *From academic education being needed for all.*
>
> **To academic education being an outdated artifact of the 20th century and before—useful for some, but no longer for all.**

Some readers will no doubt violently disagree. Many will bring up Nelson Mandela's famous quote that "Education is the most powerful weapon we can use to change the world." *But that is no longer true.* Mandela was right for his times—he lived 90 percent of his life in the 20th century, and what he said was certainly true then. But it no longer is. Today and going forward, the most powerful weapon we have to change the world is ***Empowerment,*** which, as we said, *is **Self-direction and Accomplishment with Impact**.*

The main difference from Mandela's time is that this new so-called "weapon" *IS* universal.

The key re-frame for universality is that:

> ***Every person in the world can set themselves goals and accomplish—with positive impact—on some level.***

So Why Not Just "Reform" Academic Education?

So why not make education about that? why not just "reform" academic education in this way? The reason is that it is very unlikely we can do so, and, more importantly, it is not worth the money and effort to keep trying. I believe that with the knowledge we now have, we have three options open to us in the next decade (besides doing nothing), as shown in this chart:

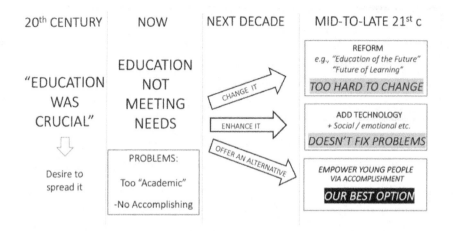

The first option is trying to "reform" or "fix" the world's existing academic education system so that it *does* work universally. This is what many are trying to do—the late Sir Ken Robinson noted, just before he died, that, "Every nation in the world is trying to reform its education in some way." Yet I believe this is impossible to do successfully. The reason is that there are too many barriers:

BARRIERS TO "REFORMING" or "FIXING" 20TH CENTURY EDUCATION

Although all those trying to reform education are well-meaning, I believe they are wasting a great deal of their own and others' time and money, and not helping our young people very much at all.

And there is yet another factor: recidivism.

"Muscle Memory" Brings Educators Back

We spoke earlier of metaphorical "muscle memory"—i.e., the human desire to go back to a long-comfortable state. Many places, after making some changes go backwards—as is currently happening with "back to basics" movements arising in many places. Such recidivism is a huge barrier to lasting change. Even when people *want* change (or say they do) their "muscle memory" often prevents it. Humans have gotten so accustomed to doing "academic education" in one way—and so dependent on it for jobs, childcare, etc.--that *even when their beliefs have changed,* they still go back to the old ways. Our schools suffer enormously from this. A great many educators say they *want* change, but they keep going back to the same old structure of courses, scheduling, testing. Sadly, this is true even though—if you talk to many educators individually—they will tell you they know what they are doing is wrong. Even those parents who say they want change balk at the disappearance of old skills and measurements. The old frame for education is incredibly hard to break. I often hear even the most forward-thinking people (in other areas) say "We need to create a 'module' or 'curriculum' or 'credential' around this." When it comes to helping young people, they are squarely in the old frame of academic education, and still passing it along.

My hope for the future is that today's young people will have far less muscle memory of old procedures. But we do have to be careful. As heretical as it may sound,

> *One of the worst things we can do is to allow our 21ˢᵗ century students to become 20ᵗʰ century teachers and educators.*

If we do this, and even encourage it (as many do) the old system will never change.

Why Can't We Just "Enhance" Academic Education through Technology?

A second possible option, favored by many is to "enhance"—i.e., modify, modernize, and "scale"—the academic education system we have. The main way they try to do this—particularly in Silicon Valley, where I now live—is by adding technology. (Others advocate for other enhancements such as "social-emotional learning" or "play.")

Although the technology-enhancement approach requires great expense and much re-training, it is the route being taken by many around the world. A great many think they can both help young people and improve the world through creating and investing in so-called educational technology (often called "ed-tech.") Investment in Ed Tech is now in the tens of billions of dollars, with multiple firms eagerly promoting such investment.

Although I am a strong believer in technology's power to help in many areas, I think enhancing academic education by adding technology is a fool's errand—because it doesn't address our real problems. Those problems are, first, academic education itself—which as we know doesn't work universally for all—and second, even more importantly, that the academic education is almost totally devoid of what universally *does* work—i.e., real-world accomplishment with impact.

But a Third Alternative Exists

There is now, however, a third alternative. We can realize and accept that success at academic education benefits some, but far from all, and we can move to add something else as our 21st century mainstream for young people, that does benefit everyone. Our best alternative, I believe, is to recognize that our young people, as they enter the New Age of Empowerment, almost all need something new—something that is universal, far more open, and very different from the former, 20th century solution of academic education.

It is not a mystery. What they need has already been conceived and tried successfully. It is called **Empowerment**—and we can now go about spreading it.

The Universally Beneficial Frame

For many of today's parents or leaders, the reality that academic education— the "great hope" of so many for the world's 2 billion young people—turns out *NOT* to be the universal solution is hard to accept. However, for most of the young people who now go through it, it is abundantly clear that this is the case.

The re-frame we need regarding universality, and the new journey it implies, is:

> *From universal academic education,*
>
> **To UNIVERSAL EMPOWERMENT.**

Empowerment is the great, helpful journey for all young people in the 21st century.

What Does "Empowerment" Mean, and What Does It Look Like?

The question you may be asking is "What does this 'Empowerment' actually look like?" What *is* this alternative Prensky says we should universally be offering to all young people—if not as a replacement for academic education, at least as an equal choice?

That is the subject of the chapters that follow. For an immediate peek, without all the steps leading up to it, you can turn immediately to Chapter 17. But before that, there are some additional re-frames it will be useful for us to look at—starting with what we should *call* our young people in the future.

Harbingers

We recently saw a vision of what is coming—and possible—in those young people who *empowered themselves* when they were kept from attending school by the Covid-19 pandemic. One of these was 10-year-old Georgina Guerra in Mexico. Georgina realized (with her mother's encouragement) that while she couldn't study academically in class, she could still set personal goals and accomplish in the real world. She chose as her goal helping other young people. She began a project of creating kits of materials that could be distributed to all students in Mexico who were out of school. Young Georgina's empowering project became enormously successful and had great impact. Georgina and her work appeared on the front page of the largest newspaper in Mexico. Other organizations, including UNESCO, chose to support it and extend it to other countries. Thousands of kits were distributed.

Reflection Question

What have you seen young people accomplish that you didn't think they were capable of—but they did? What do you think they might accomplish?

Chapter 10

RE-FRAMING YOUNG HUMANS' LABELS

From {Kids, Children, Students & Learners}
to [21ˢᵗ century people who today happen to be young, and the
first generation of the New Age of Empowerment; possibly
ALPHAS]

NOW LET US CONSIDER, for a minute, the effects of labels—i.e., what we *call* our young people. One of academic education's principal contributions — certainly rarely acknowledged — was using labels to clearly differentiate and separate, the young from the adults, in their world, in terms of their "personhood." The young are "students," "learners," "children," and "kids," and the adults are "teachers" or "professors."

Full "personhood," says academic education tacitly (but rarely, if ever, out loud), is not just a function of age, as it is legally, but is restricted to the educated—i.e., those who have completed their academic education. Those who haven't are, by dint of their lack of completion, an inferior group, called "students," or, worse, "learners." First graders are lesser people than sixth graders. High school students are lesser people than college students. All are lesser people than their degree-holding teachers. In this (again tacit) academic frame, the less academic education you have, the less of a person you are.

I understand you may disagree—many would. But before you scoff, consider that this denial of personhood for the young is eerily similar to how the world framed many other groups historically. Slaves, and even non-landowners, were sometimes considered "not fully people." It is also eerily similar to how most of the world framed the 50 percent of humans who are women—i.e., as not deserving of equal participation. The unfortunate result has been to eliminate large swathes of humans from the "people" category. Today we still often use the word "citizen" as a substitute for "person," and by doing so still omit large groups from membership in the club. Few realize, I believe, that this view of personhood has applied to young people as well—and not just as a result of academia.

Since the median age in the world is now around 30, the unfortunate result is the elimination *of almost half the world* from the "people" category (just as it was with women.) True, we sometimes call some of them "young people"—but typically only when they get older.

Because this framing of young people is so widely held, we mostly don't see, or acknowledge it. But we do act on it. We very rarely put young people—or allow them—into almost any "adult" group: committees, boards, panels, conferences, and more. In fact, we rarely put them in any roles considered "of importance" anywhere—again, very much like women in the not-so-distant past. It is no excuse to say they are not "ready" because that is what we said about women—and about every group we once excluded.

People, or Not?

It is obvious that young humans differ from adult humans in many respects. But "personhood" is not among those. Sadly,

102

however, from the young people's perspective, it is too often viewed that way. And that can be quite hurtful to them.

> *Being told you're "not ready" for something— when you know you are—hurts a lot.*

Many adults today have precisely the same trouble seeing children as "people" who are equal to themselves as they do seeing *ANY* group that is different from them as "people." In the cases of race, nationality, religion, and, more recently, gender and old age— most today recognize this less-of-a-person attitude as prejudice. But with regard to our youth, we generally do not. The sad part is that the young people feel it deeply.

A Demeaning Vocabulary

Unconsciously or not, most 20th century adults see young people as *unequal* to themselves. And to make this differentiation perfectly clear, they call them (in English), "kids," "children," "students," "learners," or some other name. (Other languages have equivalents). All of these labels make the young people into inferior beings. None of these names implies "equal."

At best, some adults see young people as "humans in training." These adults create "model governments", "model UNs," and "student (-only) councils" for them. But they—and we—we don't allow them into the "real-world"—except as inferiors.

Recently some educational groups—thinking themselves more enlightened about this—have begun talking about "student voice." A recent middle east education conference subtitled itself "Generation Unmute."

But in my experience, whenever such an adult group decides that they should include some students in the conversation, invariably only the most adult-like among the students (in guess-whose perception?) are chosen. I recently virtually attended a different education online conference where the organizers were very proud of themselves for having chosen a student as the moderator. Many of the adult participants, all of whom were educators, commented that "they wanted to be like him." This was not, however, because of any youthful qualities he had, but because he was already, to them, the "perfect adult."

On the other hand, at yet another conference, this one in-person pre-Covid, I watched an 11-year-old do a fabulous job as the conference emcee, succeeding by doing by things far more in his own way. (I tell more of his story in the *Harbingers* section at the end of this chapter.) But this is extremely rare—I have only seen it once. Most adults prefer our young people, as I noted in Chapter 1, to be like us.

Aspirational Labels

We do sometimes give our young people "aspirational" labels intended to inspire them to go in certain directions. My son's third grade teacher continually addressed her class as "my little scholars." (She had gone to Princeton.) I know, she thought she was helping, but what she was actually doing was putting pressure on those students to go in a certain direction. Few, if any in that class will become "scholars"—true scholars are relatively rare in the human population. Each will become, hopefully whatever *they* want to be, not what adults label them. Young people do not need this kind of subtle pressure from adults—even when it is well-intentioned.

In my experience, it is only when students become older that the term "young people" is typically used for them. And even then, the emphasis is still squarely on the "young" part—we rarely, if ever, think of our young as "people" first.

Eventually, young people reach the status, in the language of some, of "young adults." Yet even then, they are generally considered an inferior bunch.

Why?

I believe there is an underlying reason for this: up until now "life experience" trumped everything, as we saw in Chapter 7. To be considered a peer—or even, in many cases worth listening to—you needed at least as much life experience as the other person.

So, we grouped people by age (snidely, "date of manufacture") and by year of school graduation, or projected graduation, such as "Class of 2021." Age became our proxy for experience, and as such, age became a huge determinant of where you belonged. Even today, in some cultures, your age *vis à vis* another person determines not only your status for your entire life relative to that person, but also the specific language you must use to address them—and they you.

Young People's "Handicap"

This is now all changing. Up until now it was almost always quite a handicap to be young—and in most places it still is. Not only are you smaller—and may know fewer words with which to express yourself—but there are real limits adults put on what you can do. Some of these limits, like drinking or driving, are supposed safety constraints. But many of the limits—like voting ages—are just arbitrary, based on perceived "average" behaviors and abilities—often with absolutely no checks to see what an individual can actually do, or contribute. There are many things—like running a business or making much money—that up till now young people were just *not considered capable of doing.*

The (False?) Narrative of Play

In fact, in most places, pretty much the only thing kids really *could* do on their own—and that adults let them do on their own—was "play."

Play is, of course, something young people often enjoy. Before the rise of videogames, play was generally not seen as bad for young people—and often as good for them. As many have pointed out, play may have served a useful evolutionary purpose since young animals of many species engage in it.

But play, is not—by definition—meaningful or highly valued. In recent times some adults and companies have created narratives of "play as important for young people," or—again based on observing the behavior of animals—play as a good way for them to "learn." Many think play stimulates the imagination. Some even think of play as the best part of being young. (This is possibly because it is often—but far from always—low stress.) The "play is good for kids" narrative is pushed hardest, and to the greatest extent, by—no surprise here—the world's biggest toy company, LEGO. Pushing that narrative clearly helps them sell a great many bricks and kits, and I have nothing against those, and even enjoy them. But are they in fact helping empower 21st century young people? I have my doubts.

The essence of the narrative the is high value of "imaginative play,"—i.e., play that has no object or meaning except to you. I am very much in favor of young people expanding their imagination. But it is a mistake, I believe, to think that that just playing—in ways not valued or meaningful to the world or to others—needs to be encouraged. In fact, it is the opposite. We need, in the New Age of Empowerment, to help young people put their imaginations to work in bettering others and their world.

> *Why would anyone think that the most valuable part—or even a good part—of being young is doing something that is NOT valued or meaningful to others?*

Adult Guidance?

What I often hear from adults, on the other hand, is that before young people can do anything useful or meaningful (either to them *or* to us) they need (years of) guidance, discipline, and structure from adults. Only then will they be considered contributing members of society. Only then can they become "people" or citizens. Until then, they have to be acculturated, civilized, and socialized—brought into conformance with the civilization and culture that exists.

Many, in fact, see the result of not doing this as chaos. Recently an adult completely shocked me by citing the story *Lord of the Flies* as "evidence" that this descent into chaos is factual (rather than the fictional story it is.) Adults are often afraid of young people. In many places and situations they still require young people to be "seen and not heard"—giving their opinions no value. The only "adult" things that young people *are* allowed to do—i.e., things that involve responsibility and accomplishment— typically come in the form of chores.

Good Only for the Goose

In fact, many—if not most—of the constraints that adults put on our young people are precisely the ones they are quick to shake off as just as fast as they can once they have become adults and have thus been declared self-directing "people." During the past decade I have often spoken in school auditoriums to groups of teachers—who

107

were required to come hear my talk. Almost always they sat themselves down first (and often only) on the sides and back of the room, in what I came to call the "male balding pattern." I often wondered why they did this, as it was something they would never allow their students to do. I finally realized it was because they *could*. Restrictions were for "the kids" only. As adults, they could do what they wanted.

We Only See the Outside

I believe a great many adults in the world—although certainly not all of them—*do* think kids are inferior. "Just look at them" some say. When we do, we see they are often smaller in size than us (on the outside), and have, obviously, been in the world a shorter time. We often see their non-conforming behavior.

But we don't see inside their minds. We *can't*, as yet—in the truest sense—although we may be getting closer. But even using the methods currently available to us for seeing inside minds—such as asking—we rarely ever try. Aside from testing on or asking about the subject matter of classes, adults—including parents and teachers—rarely ask young people they meet questions beyond "What's your favorite subject?" (typically a 4-5 answer multiple choice) or "What do you want to be when you grow up?" (a question fast becoming more and more meaningless.) We rarely—if ever—ask them "Who are you? What are your dreams? Why are you unique and special?"

And if we ever do try, we often use language they don't fully understand, like "What is your passion?"—to which many answer, honestly, "I don't know." But then we too often just accept that answer—as if it were *not* the case that *every* young person has things they care deeply about. Inside, I believe, all young humans *do know*, at some level, who they are and what they care about—and most would generally love for someone to notice. As part of my talks around the world I used to conduct student panels, during which I interviewed hundreds of students of all ages. Almost all said they felt largely unlistened to, unheard, and unknown by the adults around them.

Adding Value

One particular thing we almost never ask young people—in whatever words—is "How do you—or can you—add value to our world?" Not that they can always articulate an answer. But they already know what it is that they can do better than most others around them. They know what special things someone who needs help would be well-advised to call upon *them* to do.

Today's Young People Know, and Can do, Far More Than We Think

Almost any adult who looks and listens closely to young people, of any age, concludes that they know far more than we typically give them credit for. I've always liked Alison Gopnik's metaphor for young people, *The Scientist in the Crib*. [15] The trouble is, with all our old beliefs getting in the way, we rarely look inside the crib—or wherever the young people are—and listen to them closely enough to see it.

If we do take the trouble, we will find that young people frequently, know—and will tell us—that they can do *far more* than they are generally required, or asked to. They want to be challenged—but in the right ways for them, not for us. One of the best, and rarest things we ask a young person to do is "surprise me."

No Longer a Handicap

In the New Age of Empowerment being young—formerly a handicap—has now become in many ways an advantage.

I believe

> **All young people in the 21ˢᵗ century, regardless of their age, have great advantages over young people in the past— and over the people of the 20ᵗʰ century.**

I first began noticing this around the year 2000, and wrote about it in an article entitled "Digital Natives, Digital Immigrants." [16] Even at that time big differences were clear to me. "Our students have changed radically," I wrote, "Today's students are no longer the people our educational system was designed to teach." Two decades later, what was once a handicap is fast becoming an advantage in many places—and will soon be one for all. Our youth are becoming more powerful people than we were. It is time we not only re-framed them but re-named them as well.

The needed "labeling" re-frame for our times is

> *From calling them "kids," "children," "students," or "learners,"*
> *—terms that are no longer useful—,*
>
> **To calling them "People who happen to be young"**
> —and finding a new single-word term for them.

Why?

What makes me say that these people—although they happen to be young—are so much more powerful than people (i.e., today's adults) used to be at their age? As we enter the second quarter of the 21st century (which is when I am writing) is this really true?

I believe it is, and surprisingly, perhaps, one thing that makes them more powerful is *just being born in the 21st century* (which makes them all, in my terms, "digital natives.") Why would that alone make a difference?

Because of the worldwide environment of their time.

Twenty years ago, when I first introduced the term Digital Native, there was considerable pushback around who was and who wasn't one. Many people thought that it depended on how much a person knew about digital technology. But clearly, your date of birth didn't *automatically* determine how much technology knowledge you had; many adults knew far more about technology, back then, than many young people did. Some of the adults thought that because they knew more, they were "natives" too. Others claimed that even the idea that there *were* digital natives was a myth.

But it is not a myth—at least as I see it. What has since become increasingly clear to me is that the power from being a 21st century-born "digital native" comes not from the amount you know about technology. It comes, rather, from the 21st century environment and world in which you grew up, and the often-subtle beliefs and attitudes that that has provided you. A later-in-life immigrant to a place—or an environment—may come close, but will never have all the growing up internalizations of a person born and raised there. Those difficult-to-articulate internalizations can make people live and work very differently—which is one reason we now see many intergenerational problems in our workplaces. When a company today advertises for digital native workers, as many do, they are acknowledging this. "Digital natives," today, has become a euphemism for "people who happen to be young." Some would call hiring based on this distinction a form of age discrimination. (This is something which I, ironically, having gotten older, have experienced.) I will not wade into the "ageism" discussion here, except to say that I believe that, culturally, age distinction is meaningful—and not just frivolous or a matter of semantics.

Are There Physical Differences?

On the outside, 21st century human bodies still look very much the same as they have in centuries before—aside from dress and body adornments. Whether 21st century-born brains are different from 20th century-born brains is something we may never truly know, as did not have the same measuring tools in previous times, and so do not have a good enough baseline for comparison. Some researchers try to get around this by looking at remote populations, but those may not be directly, or sufficiently, comparable to draw the conclusions we need.

But what scientists *have* finally come to understand in the early 21st century is that our environment has far more influence than previously thought on our actual biology. That influence comes through different environmental factors' affecting how our genes make (or don't make) certain proteins (i.e., how the genes "express" based on environmental factors.) The now-robust study of this process is known as "epigenetics."

Earlier in my lifetime, epigenetics was scorned by many scientists—I clearly remember being told, by mainstream neuroscientists, that Lamarck (who pioneered the field) was wrong, and that epigenetics was "crazy." But it is now generally accepted that the human body—including the brain—works differently in different environments, expressing some genes and inhibiting others. It is, as well, also generally accepted that the 21st century global environment of all young people is very different—different even for those who haven't fully "caught up" in terms of access to technology. And many see that environment affecting young people.

In fact, the pendulum has now swung the other way, as often happens. I recently heard a neuroscience practitioner worrying that the general public had gone from thinking "our genome controls everything" to thinking "the environment controls all."

The truth, of course, is in-between. We have always known that both nature and nurture determine who individuals are. We are just now learning more about why and how. The world's neuroscience understanding is still in its infancy, but it is now clear both that environmental factors have a big role to play, and that our young people live in a new environment.

Alphas—A New Kind of People

I therefore suggest, based on my own observations, that the humans born after the year 2000, roughly speaking, can be usefully re-framed, in broad historical terms, as the start of a "new kind of people." (I know am not alone in this view.) And they therefore need a new name.

The main difference which leads me to re-frame these young people as a "new kind" is not any change to their biology (which may or may not have occurred.) It is, rather, their *new capabilities* along with their *new beliefs*. Both of these have already changed demonstrably and dramatically in many places—and they are currently in the process of changing everywhere. Through these changes we have begun "hacking ourselves" (as Yuval Noah Harari puts it [17])—even before new biological techniques like cloning and gene manipulation fully arrive—creating a new kind of humans.

In this process, the sharp adult/child distinction is becoming less and less meaningful than it was in the past—and in many cases less and less relevant. People who happen to be young today cannot

113

always be so usefully distinguished from adults by their age, experience, or external appearance as were those of the past, and cannot—and should not— be so easily excluded from "adult" doings.

Different Generational Frames

Today, clear differences in perspective *vis à vis* youth have emerged between people born in the 20th versus the 21st centuries—the two generations often see the exact same young people through completely different frames and lenses. For example, many 20th century-born teachers still see, and treat, the students in their classroom as the students they remember being, or having taught, in the past. They think of their students as being the same as they (the teachers) were at that age. In reality, however, today's students are actually, in more and more places and cases, *symbiotic empowered hybrids, all networked together.*

That is truly different. And it is time we all took advantage of it.

"People Who Happen to Be Young" or "Alphas"?

Remember, the choice of appropriate frames is based on usefulness. It is almost useless—to the students and to us—to see them as what we once were—i.e., "people in training." For maximum usefulness, I believe we must now put our emphasis far more on our common "personhood," while taking advantage of the new changes

I therefore recommend that we stop referring to the people born after 2000 but not yet adults, as kids, children, students, or learners. I suggest we start referring to them as *newly empowered people who happen to be young*. The phrase may not trip off your tongue the way the single words do—but it is far more accurate. A new word for them, however, would be extremely convenient and useful.

One person I know [18] has already been calling them "Alphas"—i.e., the first (i.e., "alpha") generation of the New Age of Empowerment—and the start of a new kind of generation to come. In this usage, alpha takes on a new meaning: away from the current usage by some of "top individual in a hierarchy" *to **anybody, male or female, born in the 21st century.*** So we can say "a classroom full of alphas" "a team of alphas," a mixed team of older people and alphas."

Do you like this? I do.

I find it ironic that, as I write this, many are currently talking about "Gen Z"—the last letter in the alphabet. It is time for a new alphabet for a new Age (and time to drop the term "Gen.") We are now in a world beginning to be filled by Alphas. Let's accept and celebrate it (or find a better one-word term—I am open to suggestions.)

As we do, we will almost certainly do far better by putting our emphasis less on the "youthful" facets of these Alphas (which although true, is less relevant), and far more on the truth that Alphas are *people*—albeit with new capabilities. They are certainly equal in personhood status to adults—and perhaps even better in some ways. (This thinking is, of course, profoundly counter-cultural in many places.)

The "Other" Ageism Bias

"Ageism" is usually thought of as applying to older people—and when it is, it is clear bias to most. That we too often keep youth down

115

(i.e., "in their place") is a bias we are often blind to. Ageism should be a seen as just as much of a bias when applied to treating younger people differently as well.

"But they are kids!"

"But they are kids," you might say. "We know them—we all WERE them." "Kids can't — [fill in your own blank here—think, act, accomplish, etc.] —like adults." The trouble with that is, that in their new Age of Empowerment, in many ways they CAN—*we just don't let them*. People who happen to be young—all of them—are rarely given credit for what they CAN do. They have been doing it from birth. We adults may be caring for them, but they are doing the *same amount of thinking* as us, maybe even more.

That Pesky Pre-Frontal Cortex

One thing neuroscientists can and do observe—and have come to some consensus on—is that the pre-frontal cortex of the brain develops principally after birth, slowly, not reaching full development until roughly the early 20s. There is less consensus, however, on exactly what this means.

Many associate it with nature's building, as we get older, our so-called "executive functions," including limiting, as we get older, our propensity to take risks. (Teens are notoriously prone to risk taking.) Many see this as a positive evolutionary development for human passage into adulthood—and it may very well have been, in a survival sense, at one time.

But I have often wondered whether this late development of the pre-frontal cortex in humans—distinguishing young people from

116

adults in this physical sense—is something that is perhaps less useful in times like our upcoming future, because that future calls for more experimentation than experience. If my interpretation is accurate, (and at this point it is just speculation) it means that the very thing that made adults "better" in some sense—i.e., more developed "executive function" and control—may no longer do so in the New Age of Empowerment. The people who happen to be young in these times may be the ones with a "brain advantage"—by virtue of their *less-developed* pre-frontal cortex—over fully developed adults. Again, this is just a hypothesis, and I'm sure it will be disputed—but disputing it is part of the re-framing we need. Stay tuned.

Re-Framing Intergenerational Listening

An additional needed part of reframing our youth is re-framing—and truly understanding—what "listening to them" means. In educational conversations or gatherings, for example the only thing adding a "student voice" or "youth voice" results in, often, is adults' being told, and then taking no (or little) action. It is, too often, listening only in name. (I know this because frequently I ask the young people directly, and they often tell me.) From the young people's perspective, listening is rarely done fully enough, because to them it means that it actually leads to meaningful change—not just on the margins where it matters less, but in matters of substance.

Why is this so often the case? First, we need to look at *which* young people get listened to and heard. Hearing the truth of many of the young peoples' points of view is hard, and often unwelcome for adults. As a result, they typically choose to hear the opinions of only those few deemed—by the adults who choose them—worthy, or mature enough, to be listened to. For most of the student panels I conducted after my talks I was offered only the most conforming, high achieving students (i.e., the "best")—chosen by the educators to both show off and confirm their biases. This made it hard for the teachers to hear the full spectrum of what the young people had to say. (Occasionally, either the choosers or the students slipped up, and true messages got through. It was always eye-opening when this happened—like the girl who told a room of 5,000 Catholic school teachers in Spain (mostly nuns and priests) "We need you to respect us more."

It is very rare to see adults in power giving up their old ways in order to implement new ones that young people suggest—other than in ways that are trivial. My experience is that most Alphas do not expect this to ever happen. And they are generally right. Most adults see young people clearly as inferiors.

What Do the Alphas Expect from Adults?

My sense is not much. Recently I heard one 10-year-old girl praising a new after-school program she was attending as a place where she could "be herself." That made me wonder who she is— and who all of our Alphas are—the rest of the time.

My own listening tells me that these Alphas don't want to be on "councils"—or even just to be asked about their opinions while sitting on a stage (for most, even this, when I did it, was a first-time experience.) Nor do they want to negotiate and compromise with adults over rules they see as arbitrary, and mostly benefitting the adults.

What I hear from them, more and more, is that people who happen to be young are starting to see that they live in an Age of Empowerment. They want opportunities to accomplish whatever is meaningful to *them*, not meaningful to others. In short,

> *They want to be seen as people—*
> *and as Empowered people as well.*

The phrase "empowered people who happen to be young" may be a long one, but it at least accurate for the future. Hopefully, a shorter term one—perhaps it will be "Alphas"— will soon begin to be used.

Harbingers

A couple of years ago I encountered 10-year-old Brayden Bent, a true young person of the future, at a conference in Dubai. For three days he emceed the entire conference in front of 3000 adult attendees. Brayden, introduced as "an Internet hit, a presenter and a blogger," was better at holding the audience than most adults I have seen in the role. At one point he conducted a highly professional on-stage interview with an 11-year-old Rohingya refugee. I have rarely been so impressed or seen the future more clearly.

Reflection Question

What do *you* call (or think we should call) empowered people who happen to be young? Will you now change the label(s) you give them? Will that cause your actions to change?

PART III

RE-FRAMING LEARNING and SKILLS FOR THE FUTURE

2 Key Re-frames

RE-FRAMING LEARNING

From {an End in Itself} to [a Means for Accomplishing]

and

RE-FRAMING SKILLS

From {Basic, hard-soft & 21stc.} to [Task-Specific & 'Diamond TLC']

THERE ARE TWO RE-FRAMINGS which I want to give special and individual attention to, and highlight, because my perspectives really are extremely different from those in the mainstream. I want to re-frame now both "learning" and "skills" for the future. I discuss each of them in the next two chapters.

Chapter 11

RE-FRAMING "LEARNING"

From {an End in Itself}
to [a Means for Accomplishing]

so that our young people advance

From {being just Students and Learners}
to [being Accomplishers]

TODAY, WHEN A HUMAN CHILD REACHES A CERTAIN AGE—typically 5 or 6 in many places—if they are in a place, or family, that offers or requires school (which most, but not all are)—their main task, and goal, becomes, officially, "learning."

As living creatures, of course, they have been learning all their lives, but up until then it was rarely, if ever, a conscious, specific goal for them. Suddenly it is. "What did you learn in school today?" is the standard parental question, probably asked of kids hundreds of millions of times around the globe every day.

I think it is crucial for our young people's future that we rethink and re-frame for them this now-very-universally-accepted prime task, and goal, of learning. It is not that we don't *want* young people to learn—of course we do. We just no longer need or want them to make "learning" either an onerous task or their prime objective.

The Hardest Re-Frame of All

Based on the conversations I have, my re-frame of "learning" is perhaps the most controversial of all the re-frames in this book. It will be, for many, the hardest to accept. It is very different from the mainstream view of most educators, parents, and politicians. If you have never encountered this perspective before, it will likely require some serious reflection on your part. But I believe the implications of this re-frame are important and profound—and, far more importantly, extremely more empowering to young people.

The Re-Frame: Learning is not an End

My re-frame has to do with the role, and value, of "learning" as young people at the start of the 21st century grow up. I do not mean the learning that happens automatically as we go through the world. I mean, rather, the formalized, deliberate learning of material (i.e., curriculum), in advance of putting it to use some day—i.e., the kind of learning that usually happens in school.

Currently much of the world is convinced that this learning—formally learning specific things—is possibly *THE* most important thing for young people be doing. Some would say, even, for *all* people: "Lifelong learning" is currently a huge meme (a phrase invented, I believe, as a "long-employment-act" by those who offer it.) It is important, however, to understand that

> **The reason such learning is considered so important today by people from the 20th century is because it WAS so important in the 20th century—i.e., in those people's time.**

122

But times have now changed. I am convinced that the biggest reason 20th century education is becoming much less effective in the 21st century *is its fixation on "learning" as its goal and end*.

20th century education sees learning as what humans growing up (and those helping them grow up) should focus on and measure, and whose effectiveness we should be trying—above all—to improve. (This is often referred to as improving "learning outcomes.") Today that improvement is not an easy task. The "learning business"—which is where most of those responsible for education typically see themselves—is very much in flux.

Some argue that because the world is changing, such formal learning is even more important than it was in the past. But I propose, rather, that the changes in the world make it imperative that we put our primary focus on something different.

In my view,

The biggest flaw in 20th century education — which consists almost entirely of some form of academic education — is that it has "learning" as its primary and most important goal.

In our 20th century education, learning is what people (young and old) are expected to do. It is what is measured (or, rather, what we try to measure.) It is the result for which we give high marks and degrees. "Learning" is what education tries its hardest to produce. But why? To what end?

The Real Goal

Learning may *seem,* at first, like not only a reasonable and correct goal, but a very useful one for young people. Humans, after all, do constantly "learn" from the world around them, and some people certainly wind up having a lot more learning, overall, than others. So, learning more, many conclude, must be better. It may, in some cases, lead to more earning power.

But is doing more formal learning, by itself, and for many years, a goal worth pursuing? A question rarely asked is "What is the opportunity cost of doing this?"

In this regard we have been shaped, I believe, ("brainwashed" if you will) by education's, and academia's, perspective and marketing. I, myself, was taken in for a long time—several of my earlier essays and books are about better "learning solutions." Most academics—including most schoolteachers—see themselves as being in the learning business. What you are paid to do in that business is clear—increase learning in your students (and certainly not accomplishment, which comes, if it does, only later.)

Sadly, even when educators see the learning not happening—or worse, when they understand (as many do) that it is not what their students want or need—very few are willing give up, or even re-consider, learning as their end goal. Most are not about to switch to a different goal or business. For one thing, being in the learning business guaranteed lifetime employment—if not the highest income—for those who went into it. This was true because for a long time there were no equally good alternatives to school for young people. But now, the learning business is becoming less and less effective. And, as we shall see, good routes to adulthood other than spending many years learning in school are emerging. We are already starting to see teacher shortages in some places—a harbinger, I believe, of what is to come.

Can We "Re-define" Learning?

The thesis of this book that Real-World Accomplishment with Impact—and not formal learning—is now required by young

124

people. Perversely, some in the learning business—in order to be able to say they actually *do* produce what is actually wanted and needed—choose to re-work their definition of learning. When I suggest that Real-World Accomplishment with Positive Impact is the *real* goal—as I do in this book—those people tell me "Oh yes, learning, to me, *really means* accomplishing."

And it may, to them.

But accomplishing is *not* what learning means to most of the world, in our current times and context. "Learning" means— in our current school context that we put all young people through— *academic* learning. Academic learning is what we have today, and it is academic learning that is no longer working well. For that reason, I believe it is it is far better to re-frame our goal, going forward, in a different way.

The new "learning frame" we need for the New Age of Empowerment is:

> *From seeing "formal learning" as a worthwhile end in itself (and something necessary to do in advance),*
>
> **To seeing formal learning ONLY AS A MEANS to accomplishing useful things in and for the world.**

When viewed as a means, some formal, academic learning can be very useful and worthwhile. But when viewed as an end, it is neither useful nor worthwhile for most people.

> **In life, outside of academic school, learning is not a *goal*, but rather a *by-product* of existing and doing.**

We Can Stop Making This Critical Mistake

Making learning itself an end goal is a crucial mistake we have inherited from the academics and continued to retain. For the New Age of Empowerment to actually be empowering for young people, I highly recommend we stop prioritizing learning (of the school kind) as the goal for our young people—and, in fact, for all people. We should focus people instead on *real-world accomplishment*: i.e., on people getting positive and useful things done in their world—not someday, but now. And we should begin viewing whatever learning happens in the process of accomplishing—as it inevitably does—as merely an added by-product and benefit.

Importantly, this DOES NOT mean that we should think only about jobs, or vocational education—an oft-heard criticism from academics. The truth is

> **One can focus on real-world accomplishment in every context—even in the most liberal of the liberal arts.**

We just don't.

Strange?

If you ever attended (or worked in) a school, this new frame of "learning as not the product but the by-product" may seem quite strange. In that once-useful frame, learning is the goal *because it is assumed that formal learning is something you need to do before you can accomplish anything useful.* Formal learning, in that frame, is the *required pre-requisite* for accomplishing. Most employers want to know, before they hire you, that you have spent years learning—and getting high marks for it—as "evidence" that you can accomplish. Because formal learning involves almost no

126

accomplishment, even though the results are mixed they had little else to go on. Even today many employers—still using the old frame—often want to see your academic degree(s) before they will even talk to you.

School Shaped Our Perspective

But that is a completely "school-shaped" perspective. If you happen to be someone who didn't go to school (or much school) your perspective will very likely be different. In your mind, you *know* you have certain capabilities—although they might not be the academic capabilities school values—and you know there are things you can accomplish—and you want the opportunity to show them. What others learned in school doesn't matter for success—school is just a convenient—though often painful—signaling system. In our old frame, as professor Bryan Caplan has perspicaciously written [19], school, and all the learning one does there that culminates in a degree, really just signal three things to an employer: (1) that you can do reasonably complex work, (2) that you can stick to a task until it is completed, and (3) that you are capable of doing things you don't want to, but that others require of you. *What* you learned is of little or no consequence.

It is this last point—doing something you don't want to—that is now causing many of the problems. That is very much what the old frame required. But young people increasingly perceive a new frame, in which they are far freer. They are less and less willing to comply in school because they know they increasingly don't have to in order to succeed in life.

The young people's new frame is not learning, but ***becoming Empowered.***

The 21st Century Difference

The two big differences in the New Age of Empowerment are that (1) the signal that you can things you don't want to is now less necessary in life—because there are so many new alternatives for doing something you want to, and (2) almost all the learning now done in school—almost entirely from and about the past—*is no longer even necessary, in many cases, to do what you **DO** want to.* (And, if and when it is, it can now be done far more quickly and efficiently on your own.)

Learning by Doing?

Humans—like all living thing—do learn, every minute of every day, based on changes in their environment. Even non-humans, such as plants do this. The difference is that they learn almost entirely *as a result of* what they do, not in advance of it. Non-humans have no formal classes, yet they have ways of passing their learning to others—typically through accomplishment (e.g., surviving, growing taller or stronger.)

But, you may ask, isn't the formal learning process humans have developed an advantage here?

Probably in the past it was—when young people had so much less access to experience and information. But the learning that really counts—that proves valuable in life, work, and survival, and that every human, animal, and plant people needs, comes NOT through classes, or even just through doing, but through *accomplishing*.

I am sure some may say that all I am advocating is "learning by doing"—which is certainly nothing new. But I am actually opposed to using "learning by doing" as a slogan or frame—because it again makes the goal "learning." It is learning—even by doing—that is

NOT A GOOD ENOUGH GOAL for today's and tomorrow's young people. What people in the New Age of Empowerment need—and what we are after—is accomplishing (i.e., succeeding at getting something done) in the real world. That is what I advocate.

Not all "doing" succeeds or results in accomplishments we are proud of. Failure along the way is often part of the process, and understanding what doesn't work, or hasn't worked, can also be part of that process. But, importantly, *learning what hasn't worked no longer requires years of school.* Nor do I think we should be celebrating our failures, as some—including many who advise entrepreneurs—advocate. I believe what we should celebrate instead is only *whatever eventual accomplishment grows out of the failures.* It is not the means we should glorify, but rather the end we seek.

Today's Formal Learning is Mostly a Big Waste of Time

Today, because there are so many new ways to find the things you need when you need them, most of the formal learning we have our young people do in advance of accomplishing is a huge waste of their time—as many of them try (usually without success) to tell us. Almost all of it is a vestige and artifact of the past—of the 20th century and before—when the world was far more repetitive, when accomplishment by young people was nearly impossible, and when things they needed in order to accomplish were very difficult to find. In that old context it made sense to learn a bunch of possibly-useful things up front.

But today's context is different. Young people increasingly live in a world where they need to invent, using the new ideas and the latest materials. Theirs is now a world where—when they want to address a situation or problem—they can easily form teams, explore solutions, check what others have done, implement their idea, and iterate as they go, and get something done—i.e., accomplish.

Since accomplishing—i.e., getting something done—is *so much easier* in the New Age of Empowerment, doing anything *other* than that is a waste of precious time.

Today we should be taking the term "recreation" literally—as re-creation. Previously, we *had* to do formal learning in advance because we were almost always building incrementally and what we needed from the past was not easily findable when we actually needed it. But now it is readily available—as are the ways to use it. And while we still build on work others have done, the past work we need to use is often far more recent. Therefore,

> **The very best preparation a young person can get today is accomplishment in the real-world—with positive impact— in whatever area interests them at the moment, and NOT spending years learning in advance.**

I often hear adults counter this with "Wait—Don't you want your doctor (or surgeon) to have gone to years of medical school?" My answer is "not necessarily." I certainly want a *good* doctor, and in the past, listening to years of in-class lectures might have been a way to become one. But not tomorrow—or even today, necessarily, because things now change too fast. The Dean of Harvard Medical School now tells his incoming students that "by the time you graduate 50 percent of what we teach you will be obsolete or no longer relevant." [20]

Today, for *any* doctor, it's better to first check the Internet for updates—even since your last appointment. Today, as a patient, it's wiser to rely, if available, on a machine or robot for anything routine. The surgeons' motto during war in the past, was "see one, do one, teach one." Now any doctor or budding doctor can, remotely, from their mobile phone, watch the best expert(s) in the world either live-streamed or on YouTube, virtually assist another physician doing a procedure while asking questions, do an operation him or herself (with or without a machine they supervise) and then post the whole thing on You Tube, with comments, for others. if one is connected, "See one, do one, teach one" can be done from anywhere. Every medical student or doctor can call up—as collective statistics or individually—the results from millions of similar patients. A human doctor is really now only needed for the cases that have never been seen before, where *no one* has experience. "Experience, as writer Keven Kelly says, "is overrated."

Is Lived Experience Even Necessary?

Now, in our young people's times, there is no longer the same need to "gather experience." Even before young humans are of what we today call "school age, if there is something they like and want to do, they can begin seeing others do it—and doing some of it themself in a very close simulation. (This still currently depends on where they live and their circumstances, but it is coming soon to all.) Therefore spending years learning in advance in school—even for things they love and want to learn about— takes up time that could be far better spent on real-world projects they choose.

It is widely known that when people are forced to learn formally, most of what they learn will be forgotten—quickly or eventually. Now that everything is quickly findable precisely when one needs it, even *re*-finding something is often a waste of time, because it is likely to have changed. So, the only things a person now needs to keep "in their head" are the things they use every day (with frequent updating)—because they may still speed your work up—along with some general principles and guidelines. Most of both are best acquired not from classes you once took, but from accomplishment.

Being a Full-Time Student is Obsolete

So, in the New Age of Empowerment—even today—there is little or no need for anyone to be a full-time "student" or "learner."

Some now cite "learning to learn" as an important thing to do, and, certainly, various techniques can certainly make learning more efficient. But it is often trivial to learn these techniques—i.e., by watching a few You Tubes. Moreover, unlike in the past, the best methods are continuously changing. I have long had an app in mind for increasing judgment rapidly in any area.

Whatever new learning *is* needed to accomplish something—and of course some typically is—it can *always* be done more efficiently on the fly, as needed. My son successfully flew a small plane for the first time with no formal training whatsoever—he had watched many You Tubes, practiced on his simulator software, and for safety had an instructor with him to correct any mistakes. There will always be "Oh no, what do I do now?" situations, despite any amount of experience—and having an experienced human guide next to you is a nice—but often expensive—way, but we now have more ways to deal with unforeseen events than just a person with years of past expertise. Assuming I had a device with a fast enough connection, I could probably even learn how to open a parachute I grabbed as I jumped out of a burning plane before I landed.

Once a person has access to today's current technology—and by the mid-to late 21st century that is highly likely to be everyone—that person, carries with them access to all the best experts, instructors, and coaches in the world, and we are getting far better at parsing it. Today that access typically comes via a smartphone. But by the time today's young people grow up it will likely come directly into their brain. Why would anyone, then, need years of formal learning?

The young people who currently have access to technology already operate thus way in many domains—videogaming is just one example. The hard part is getting people from the past to believe it is true. It is those adults who need to re-frame "learning" for the 21st century world:

> *From learning being something you need to do in advance,*
>
> **To learning being just an as-needed part of accomplishing useful, positive things in the real-world.**

The Real Goal in an Empowered World Should Always Be Accomplishing

Although academics may say otherwise, the main reason humans did (and still do) formal learning in advance was to accomplish useful things. That—accomplishing a goal you set— is the real goal for most humans. In fact, most people don't even *like* doing any learning that they haven't initiated themselves for a purpose—learning just for pleasure is the pastime of very few. The few who do like learning for its own sake often become teachers—which is why so many of them talk about instilling a love of learning in their students.

The young people know, when they hear teachers say this, that the acronym for Love of Learning is "LOL."

For some, the purpose of learning might be—as the scouts say—to "be prepared." That may be useful in situations where time is of the essence. But do you need to learn *everything* in advance? How much in-advance practice does one need?

133

What *About* Practice?

We all know that to get good at something that doesn't change it helps to do it again and again. We also all know that such "practice" is almost always repetitive and boring. So how much "practice" do our young people still need?

Most often we practice because someone makes us do it. But people do practice *on their own* when they have an accomplishment goal in mind. They practice golf swings to get lower scores and beat their friends or boss. They practice questions to get a high exam score to get into the university they want to attend. They practice skills (be they welding or stock trading) to get jobs. They practice techniques, like design thinking, because they want to create products that sell.

The saying, in English, is "practice makes perfect." But neuroscience provides an important re-frame:

> *From practice makes perfect,*
>
> **To practice makes permanent.**

Repetitive practice builds up strong neural connections in our brain, which then become what neuroscientists call "zombie" circuits. This is enormously useful in some situations, like performing music, because it lets fingers do their repetitive job as the conscious brain concentrates on other things like the shape of the melody and the connection with the audience. But it is also what causes us to drive directly home when we meant to stop at the store. "Zombies" (and worse, "zombies that are wrong") are less and less what 21st century people need to be. We now have symbiotic machine parts for that—often far easier to re-program when necessary. Humans are best when fully conscious and/or thinking hard. This implies that ONLY practicing the RIGHT thing over and over is productive—being even slightly off can be dangerous.

It's Not "Learning by Doing" We Need

I want to conclude this chapter on learning with this reminder:

What empowers young people is **NOT** "learning for its own sake," or "practicing, over and over," or "learning by doing,"

What empowers young people is
"ACCOMPLISHING—and (ideally) learning in the process."

Harbingers

Early examples of this new re-framing of learning include every player of videogames now in the world. All acquired the complex skill of gaming with no formal classes, no need to earn a degree, no desire to sit and practice, but with only a desire to accomplish one thing—WIN!

Another early example is Gitanjali Rao—named Time Magazine's "Kid of the Year" in 2020 (note the old-frame language.) When she really wanted to accomplish a goal, she went and found precisely the knowledge she needed, without having to go through years of academic training. When Gitanjali was 11, she heard that the people in Flint, MI (USA), had a problem with poisonous lead concentrations in the tap water—and that there was no easy way for those who were possibly affected to test for it. So she set herself a goal of developing an easy-to-use test to people check their own water. She had a hunch she could use a new carbon nanotube technology she had read about. But as she reports in her book, *A Young Innovator's Guide to STEM*, [21] "I was not a chemistry expert AT ALL." She found a few simple videos online that explained ionic and covalent bonds in an easy-to-accept format. She reviewed a single online course, and she took a tour of a local nanomaterial manufacturer to learn more about the chemical compositions of carbon nanotubes. "I did not even bother to memorize the whole periodic table because I did not have to!" she writes. "I had learned enough to keep going." That is what is coming.

Reflection Question

Do you think you can change your beliefs about how important "learning in advance" (i.e., in school), is for young people? Do you want to?

Re-framing Growing Up

Re-framing learning as a means and not an end will help us re-frame the whole "growing up" process to make much more sense in the New Age of Empowerment. (I do that in Part IV of this book.)

In the new growing-up process young people no longer need to spend so much time mastering whatever it is we decide to teach them. They can spend the time, rather, in understanding themselves, setting their own positive goals (with adults' help), and learning only—or principally—what they need to accomplish them.

Even without the kind of education we try to give them today, future young humans will, because of the world they live in, be far more knowledgeable and informed than young people were in the past. And, in the new frame, young people will be freer—much freer than they are in school today—to pursue any (non-destructive) thing in life that interests them and produces positive results. I look at the new growing up process in Part IV. But before we do that, a word on Skills.

136

RE-FRAMING HUMAN SKILLS

From {Basic, Hard-Soft, and 21st c.}
To [Task-Specific and 'Diamond TLCs']

OUR YOUNG PEOPLE DO NEED SKILLS. But which skills do they need in the New Age of Empowerment, and how will they get them? That is what I re-frame in this chapter.

The Old Frame

The old frame for skills, still is still very much in use, is an arcane mix of "basic," "hard" and "soft," plus, more recently, some relabeling as "21st century."

"Basic skills," in this old frame, are those we think everyone needs to possess, and that we try to give people early in life. (I re-frame what these basic skills are for the New Age of Empowerment in Chapter 12.) "Hard skills" are those requiring specific knowledge that can be taught in a curriculum—the ones each person needs depends on the job that person has. "Soft skills" are the skills—sometimes referred to as "people skills"—around human interaction in all contexts. (While helpful to all, these are often lacking in many.) Sills, in the old frame are also sometimes classified into "academic" (i.e., "for thinking") and "practical" (i.e., for "doing").

More recently, we are hearing about "21st century skills" (which is, really just a selection from the above.)

A New Frame for Skills

I suggest there is a new and better way to re-frame human skills for the New Age of Empowerment:

From classifying skills as basic, hard, soft, and 21st century,

To classifying skills as either "Task-specific" or "Diamond TLCs"— i.e., Transferable Lifetime Capabilities.

Task-specific skills, like tasks themselves, are limitless and extremely varied. One very good piece of good news is that in the New Age of Empowerment most of them can already be—or will be able to be—acquired online. I will therefore not focus here on those. I will focus in this chapter mostly on the Diamond Skills—also known as "Transferrable Lifetime Capabilities," or "TLCs."

Transferrable Lifetime Capabilities (TLCs)

The TLCs are lifetime in two senses. First, all of them can take a lifetime to master. And second, whatever pieces of them are acquired along the way generally *last* a lifetime. These skills are, in a sense, "harder than hard." I therefore call them "Diamond Skills" or "Diamond TLCs." Here is a chart (not necessarily exhaustive) of many of them:

"DIAMOND SKILLS"			(Transferable Lifetime Capabilities)
EFFECTIVE THINKING	EFFECTIVE ACTION	EFFECTIVE RELATIONSHIPS	EFFECTIVE ACCOMPLISHMENT
Understanding Communication	Habits of Highly Effective People	Communication & Collaboration	Insistence & Focus on MPI (Measurable Positive Impact) and Value
Quantitative & Pattern Thinking		- One-to-one	
Scientific Thinking	Body & Health Optimization	- In teams	
Historical Perspective	Agility	- In families	
Problem-Solving (Individual & Collaborative)	Adaptability	- In communities	Completing Small & Local Projects
Curiosity & Questioning	Leadership & Followership	- At work	
Creative Thinking	Decision Making Under Uncertainty	- Online	
Design Thinking		- In Virtual Worlds	Completing Larger Projects
Integrative Thinking	Experimentation		
Systems Thinking	Research	Listening	Completing Distributed Projects
Financial Thinking	Prudent Risk-taking	Networking	
Inquiry & Argument	Reality Testing & Feedback	Relationship-building	
Judgment	Patience	Empathy	Completing Global Projects
Transfer	Resilience & "Grit"	Courage	
Aesthetics	Entrepreneurship	Compassion	Building & Maintaining Effective Teams
Habits of Mind	Innovation	Tolerance	
Positive Mindset	Improvisation	Ethics	
Self-knowledge of one's:	Ingenuity	Politics	Project Management & Agility
Dreams - Concerns - Passions- & Strengths	Strategy & Tactics	Citizenship	
	Breaking Barriers	Conflict Resolution	
Stress Control	Project Management	Negotiation	True Innovation
Focus & Sitzfleisch*	Programming Machines	Coaching & Being Coached	
Contemplation & Meditation	Making Effective Videos	Mentoring & Being Mentored	
	Innovating with current & future technologies	Peer-to-peer	
*Staying power			

Skills, or Capabilities?

Some prefer the term "capabilities," to "skills," reasoning that the term "skills" is less comprehensive, and perhaps more demeaning. Personally, I am indifferent. I refer to them as both "Diamond Skills" and "Diamond TLCs"—Transferable Lifetime Capabilities. Like the other oft-used meaning of TLC—*tender, loving care*—the Diamond TLCs are a tremendous gift we can give to our young people to empower them.

Limited in Number, but, Combinatorically Huge

Although the skills in the chart can certainly be broken down further, and one can certainly add more, an important realization for me was that these high-level lifetime capabilities are actually limited in number. In whatever way you choose to count them (and there are myriad ways), there are possibly less than a few hundred. But any single individual can only master, to a very high level, a small number of the Diamond Skills in a lifetime (they can possess several more at a below-master level). Each individual has their own, unique mix, or profile, of Diamond Skill strengths.

And how many of these unique profiles are there? When people select their own combinations and we look at the number of possible profiles, there are far more possible combinations of these skills than the number of humans who have ever lived. That, in part, is what makes us individually unique—the likelihood of two people having exactly the same profile of highly developed Diamond skills is low. It is why it is useful to put different profiles together as teams. It is when we put those different combinations of Diamond TLCs together in teams that we begin to have real power.

And They are All "Symbiotic"

And *even more* power derives from the fact that that all these Diamond capabilities are, in the New Age of Empowerment, becoming *symbiotic*—as we saw in Chapter 2.

Here is another key re-frame regarding "skills":

From thinking of "Human skills" that can be done with or without technology and, separately, "tools" to help do them better,

To thinking about, and seeing "Symbiotic Human Skills," requiring *combinations* of biological and technological parts.

The reason this particular skills re-framing is so important—and powerful—is because what people require in the New Age of Empowerment are NOT the skills in themselves, *but the ability to employ them in our new, future context*. In the New Age all of these skills be performed by humans in symbiosis in a new "hybrid" way, i.e., in symbiosis with our new technological parts and capabilities. None of these skills, I believe, will escape this, and therefore it is crucial for people who happen to be young to be thinking in these terms.

21st Century Skills?

As we noted at the start of this chapter, some have recently been re-classifying a selection of already-known skills under the new label of "21st century skills." They do this to highlight, I believe, our supposed future requirements. There are, however, several competing lists. For example,

- The World Economic Forum's list includes "complex problem solving; critical thinking; creativity; people management; coordinating with others; emotional intelligence; judgment and decision making; and service orientation."

  But it doesn't include imagining.

- Tony Wagner's list—that he calls "7 Survival Skills," although it really includes 14 (since to get to the "rememberable" number of 7 all are doubled up)— includes: Critical thinking & problem-solving; collaboration across networks & leading by influence; agility & adaptability; initiative & entrepreneurship; effective oral & written communication; accessing & analyzing information; curiosity & imagination.

  But it doesn't include emotional intelligence.

While all the slightly differing lists serve mainly as forms of the creator's "branding," there is no doubt that the skills they designate as "21st century" skills are, and will be, important—*but, importantly, so will all the others in the chart.*

All the "old" human skills don't go away in the New Age of Empowerment—and shouldn't. Neither of the lists shown here, for example, includes empathy. How important a skill will that be in the 21st century?

Also, importantly, there are no "new" skills on any of these lists—should there be? In my view, the most important 21st century skill missing from all these lists—and perhaps the most important for empowerment, is *becoming symbiotic with our technology,* as we have discussed.

Re-framing "Hard" and "Soft"

Our old classification of skills as "hard" or "soft" also badly needs re-framing. I believe this is a legacy of the U.S. military, later picked up by human resource departments in businesses. It is now often used in education as well.

Whether or not this hard/soft distinction was ever useful, it no longer is—because it gets things backwards. The confusing part is that term "hard" really means "task-specific," and not "difficult." Although hard skills may be more or less complex or difficult to master—and can be extremely specialized—they are generally diagrammable and can often be put into step-by-step manuals. Hard skills may involve some judgment, but people with the right aptitudes can generally be trained, in relatively limited periods of varying lengths, to do them. Some of them are new, such as those required for using or maintaining new, developing technology. But machines can increasingly be taught to perform many of these task-specific skills on their own.

Re-framing the "Soft Skills"

The skills that are today called "soft" may have gotten that name because they are "squishy," i.e., not easy to put hard and fast rules, or descriptions around. What has confused many here is that the term "soft" can also imply "of lesser importance"—which is certainly not true.

The skills in this "soft" category are sometimes called "people skills" because almost all involve other humans. Perhaps for this reason, they are in many cases the most difficult (i.e., "hardest," paradoxically) to acquire and master. They are also, possibly, the most valuable for humans to have, because—unlike many task-specific skills—they are "transferable," i.e., useful in a great many situations. All are complex skill sets that take a long time—often a lifetime—to fully develop. And, because they almost all involve other humans—they are not entirely replaceable by technology. All require symbiosis.

I submit this new way to re-frame what we now call "soft skills":

From calling them "soft," meaning lesser, or optional,

To calling them "Diamond TLCs"—harder-than hard—
with each individual having a different set.

Diamond TLCs

The big re-frame implied in this name change is acknowledging that these skills are *Transferable Lifetime Capabilities* **(TLCs).** They contrast sharply with task-specific skills in several ways. They are, as we noted, far more limited in number. They do not depend, like task-specific skills do, on the task you happen to be doing in any situation. In fact, in *any* situation having as many as possible, to the highest degree possible, is useful—and often necessary.

The Transferable Lifetime Capabilities are in no way new to, or specific to, the 21st century. The TLCs have been recognized, developed, and honed by humans over millennia. Nor—other than the new addition of symbiosis—are they new to the New Age of Empowerment.

Unique Profiles + Life-Long Development

While all the TLCs are useful to have, no single person can have all of them, fully developed. As noted, if we assume, that at the level in the chart, that the TLCs are roughly 100 in number, then the different ways one could have various combinations of them is many times the number of people on earth. Therefore, the probability of anyone's having a particular combination is low—especially the more skills one has. There is very large number of unique ways it could happen, which is why each individual human is likely unique in their particular mix, or profile, of skills. Each person has a unique profile of a limited number of such skills, and that is the reason—or one of the reasons—we often do better working in teams.

And, like musicianship, and performing, each TLC requires *life-long development* to get to the highest levels. That is one potential advantage of being older in the New Age of Empowerment!

Diamond TLCs

I call these Transferable Lifetime Capabilities "Diamond Skills" or "Diamond TLCs"—because they are, in a sense, "harder than hard," like diamonds. The TLCs are the life-long skills that humans have discovered and refined over the hundreds of thousands of years humans have been around. And while the number of possible combinations is immense, the individual number of Transferable Lifetime Capabilities is not so large as to be difficult to grasp.

To make grasping them even easier, I classify the Diamond Skills—or Transferable Lifetime Capabilities—into four groups: **Thinking Skills, Action Skills, Relationship Skills** and **Accomplishment Skills.** There is some overlap, and you might prefer to structure them differently. But many have found this classification useful.

Note that the list in the chart above is not exhaustive. Nor is it meant to be—there are doubtless omissions. You can add any you think should be included. Bear in mind that they are an "ideal" set. No single person has—or will ever have—all these Diamond Skills fully developed, because developing each one is a life-long process. No one should expect any person—young or old—to be good at all of them. Every person makes his or her own choices among them based on who they are, and each creates their own profile and preferences. That profile—and not one's physical appearance—is what creates each person's value-adding "uniqueness" in the world. (I describe what "value-adding" means in Chapter 18). Successful teams combine people with differing combinations of Diamond TLCs and profiles. Different teams are needed, both in composition and size, for different kinds of tasks.

All Should be "Known About" by Everyone

Yet even though no individual will ever master *all* of these TLCs to a high degree, it is important, I believe. for all young people to know that all of them exist—and roughly what they entail. They should also know that all can be best developed though use—e.g., in projects—both in their early years and throughout their lives.

Parents and other adults should help young people make a start at as many Diamond TLCs as possible—beginning with those that the young people and adult together consider most inherent in that person, and important for each project they do. The goal is to find the best "profile" of an eventual set of highly developed Diamond TLCs for each individual. That process should begin as early in life as possible.

Effective

Note that I have labelled each column in the chart "Effective" (i.e., Effective Thinking, Effective Action, Effective Relationships and Effective Accomplishment.) I have done this because all the Diamond TLCs can be possessed and used ineffectively as well. Coaching helps considerably in effectively developing these Diamond TLCs—even the best musicians and athletes often retain coaches all their careers. Peer-to-peer coaching and feedback and "mentoring" can often help as well.

Empowering

Possessing and applying as many effective Diamond TLCs as possible is extremely empowering in one's life, projects, and work. To fully succeed in the New Age of Empowerment, each person will need to find, develop, and apply, over their lifetime, their *unique profile, or combination* of Diamond TLCs, and apply their unique profile, individually and in teams, to accomplishing in the world and realizing their dreams.

The Issue of Transfer

I call all the Diamond Skills "transferrable" but what exactly does that mean? What academics call "transfer" is an important consideration when it comes to Diamond Skills. It means that if you can, using a certain skill or capability, resolve a problem about one thing, say, a car, you can also, do it with a similar problem about another thing, like an airplane, or a flower—without needing to "redeveloping" that skill anew for each specific case. Once you have learned a methodology in science, for example, you can also use it in history.

I believe that while only some task-specific skills are transferrable—say from one computer operating system to another, ALL the Diamond Skills in the above chart are, in principle, transferable (which is why I call them TLCs), The question, however, is how *automatic* is transfer? Can all young people *automatically* transfer skills or capabilities they learn in one domain to another?

Typically, the ability to transfer varies from person to person. Some do it almost instinctively, while for others transfer is a skill that needs to be acquired. Some, in order to do it—or to do it well—must be shown how, and must put in effort and practice. The degree of transferability may also vary skill from skill to skill. While we still know relatively little about transfer, we do know that transfer is a place where coaching can be very helpful.

Blind Spots

We also know that transferring skills is a place where blind spots can easily occur, even in the most facile and experienced. One of the best ways adults can help young people is to point out opportunities for skills transfer, i.e., occasions when certain skills one already has can be re-applied in new contexts—and also when they can't, and shouldn't be. We also need to be aware and remind ourselves that transfer does not happen the same way in everyone.

Harbingers

My harbingers of Diamond TLCs and skills transfer are the many young people in the world already living and working in the Cloud. They are transferring and applying all their TLCs to connect with people in new ways in this world, while at the same time mastering symbiosis and a great many new, task-specific, skills. They have also become experts in using a new form of coaching, and facilitating transfer—You Tube.

Reflection Question

What is your own unique profile of highly-developed Transferable Lifetime Capabilities? How well has that mix served you? Can you think about developing a unique mix in each young person you know?

Acquiring Diamond TLCs

How in the New Age of Empowerment, will young people obtain their task-specific and Diamond TLC skills? How can they best find their own, unique mix and profile to work on and develop? And how should they—and we—assess their progress?

That is the subject of the next section, Part IV of this book. In this section I rethink and re-frame in turn each of the various stages of a new, more empowering, process of growing up. I re-name those stages as: Starting, Expanding, and Realizing of dreams. However to make it easier to relate it to today, I name the chapters using 20th century terms: Parenting, "The Basics," The School Years, Assessment, Higher Education, and Work. Let us begin our journey.

PART IV

RE-FRAMING THE NEW 'GROWING UP' JOURNEY

Parenting, Education, & Work in the New Age of Empowerment

From {Being Directed}
to [Becoming Empowered]

Chapter 13

'GROWING UP EMPOWERED'

Re-framing the 21st Century 'Growing Up' Process

From {Being Parented, Going to School, and Working} to [Starting, Expanding and Realizing Your Dreams]

ALL THE RE-FRAMES in this book are offered in order *to help us take more appropriate and effective action in the future regarding our young people.* In Part I, I re-framed their overall new journey as becoming empowered rather than just educated. in Part II, I looked at several useful ways to re-frame their times, who they are, what they believe, what their world is like, what they should aspire to, what is universal for all of them, and what they are called. In Part III. I re-framed "Learning" and "Skills," two particularly important areas.

A New Frame for Growing Up

Now, based on all those re-framings, I consider the question:

> *How can we best frame the whole process of 'growing up' in the New Age of Empowerment?*

I do this because it helps us determine what to do with these new and different frames—i.e., the various *actions* all the previous re-frames imply we should take.

I see all those re-frames as pointing to a new era of powerful, individually-unique, but connected-and-symbiotic humans—in what I call the New Age of Empowerment. I think this will happen collectively to humanity, despite any particular action on any individual's part. But through our individual actions we can either speed up or slow down the time it takes take to fully enter the new Age.

The collective action this new Age requires, I believe, is a consensus on *a new process for growing-up*, everywhere in the world—a process that empowers the new people, currently young, of the New Age of Empowerment.

A television commercial I recently saw from the TGR (Tiger Woods) Foundation put it well:

> **"The greatest way to improve the world is to empower those who enter it."**

That means creating a more empowering growing-up process than the one we currently have. What should it look like?

The New 'Growing Up' Process

To be useful, the new process of growing up needs to move from our old and current frames for growing up to new models and frames for each of the growing-up stages.

Overall, I believe that from the adult's perspective we should re-frame the growing-up process as evolving

> From directing young people,
>
> *To Empowering Young People.*

Since much (or most) of that process is done by the young people themselves, the re-frame from their point of view is

> From being directed,
>
> *To Becoming Empowered.*

The Old 'Growing Up' Frame

Through the 20th (and early 21st) century, the overall process of growing-up was very similar almost everywhere in the world—with only the details varying from place-to-place. There are three principal, close-to-universal stages in this process: "being a kid." "going to school", and "finding a job." Each has its own form of "direction" by adults.

At various times and in various places one or more of these stages may have overlapped, been skipped, or run concurrently. But in most places the stages were:

1. "Being a Kid" — This stage consists of being raised by your parents (or a proxy) until roughly the age of 5. *During this stage adults direct young people by passing to them their personal and cultural beliefs about the world.*

2. "Being a Student" — This stage consists of going to school, to whatever extent possible, for the next 6-20 years of life. *During this stage adults direct young people by telling them what is important—i.e., their community's culture, history, and subject matter they consider worthwhile.*

3. "Finding a Job and/or Career" — This stage consists of looking for and beginning work— often work that one would keep doing in one place or another, and perhaps at more advanced levels, for most of one's life. *During this stage adults direct young people by letting them know—principally through the hiring process—what opportunities the young people have, and what they can or can't do in their particular world.*

By the end of this old process of growing-up, having been fully directed along the way, one becomes "an adult"—capable, supposedly, of joining the club of other adult people, and supporting oneself and ones' family in the world.

This old frame persists well into the 21st century, and today almost everyone is familiar with it.

A New Way

I see a big change coming in this "growing-up" frame—as young people in almost all places grow up increasingly symbiotic and connected to each other in the now quickly arriving New Age of Empowerment.

I still see three main stages, but I re-frame them as: **Starting, Expanding** and **Realizing**. In more detail:

Stage 1: Starting / Finding Deep Self-knowledge — In the new frame the first years of one's life are not just about being a kid and randomly (and ideally imaginatively) playing. The starting years are, also, more importantly, about gaining deep self-knowledge, empowering beliefs— such as "I can"—, starting to connect with others like yourself— "affinity groups"—around the world, and beginning to express your own uniqueness in future-oriented ways. One place this new first stage is already appearing is through the worldwide rise of connected online social media and gaming.

Stage 2: Expanding / Applying to Accomplishments — The next decade (or two) in the new frame are *not* about formal learning, as in the past. They are rather about expanding the starting process through accomplishing. This means continually accomplishing—in teams with complementary members from around the globe—real-world-impacting projects that *you choose* based on your unique interests and strengths. This is a period of building one's personal resume of accomplishments with a Measurable Positive Impact on one's world. It is the phase when each person starts to add unique value to their world. It is now beginning in pockets around the world.

Stage 3: Realizing — in this new stage, the combination of self-knowledge of your uniqueness, *plus* the real-world projects you have accomplished *and* the worldwide network you have built, leads to a lifetime of work that is meaningful to you and adds value to your world. *And* it leads to realizing, as much as possible, whatever dreams you had and have—however they may change along the journey. This stage continues, and continues to evolve, over one's entire lifetime. Most of the processes of this re-framed stage still need to be invented.

A Far More Useful 'Growing-Up' Frame

I remind you again that the criterion for adopting a re-frame is *usefulness*. The world's current frame for growing up—with stages in which young people are totally in need of being directed by adults all along the way—is no longer useful or helpful to them in a New Age of Empowerment. What they now need from adults to become empowered in their New Age is not direction, but rather helpful coaching and guidance.

Our old frame for growing up and raising kids—based on direction—grew out of a long age when young people grew up almost entirely in *local communities that mostly repeated and replaced what had come before.* The young people in these communities were isolated from their peers in other communities around the world, and even in their own country. They had few means of accomplishing, or even finding out what was going on in other places. *They needed direction to be able to conform and replace where they were.*

Now we see young people becoming globally connected early, getting—from almost the beginning of life—new capabilities never before imagined, and accomplishing in the real world in their earliest years. It is this new combination of connection, capabilities and accomplishment that defines the "New Frontier" and the New Age of Empowerment we are talking about.

Today, Every Old Growing-up Stage Now Fails Our Young People

The problem we are now faced with on this new frontier is that **all of the former, 20th century growing-up stages—i.e., being a kid, going to school and finding a job—are now failing our young people**. None of the stages work well in, and for, the New Age of Empowerment. The entire system no longer works, Therefore, better ways of growing up in a New Age of Empowerment are desperately needed.

Let's look at how each stage is failing our young people.

How *Parenting* Now Fails Our Young People

There are, of course, some great parents—hopefully you are among them! And there are also some horrible ones. Most are, realistically, in-between. But almost none of them know what to do with their kids in this New Age of Empowerment. As many have observed, there is no preparation or "owner's manual" for being a parent, and, if there were, it would certainly now be out-of-date. Typically, the guides are cultural norms, relatives, and mostly, as a model, your own experiences—positive or negative—growing up. Despite some experiments and some collective cultural behaviors, up until now the parenting stage was pretty much left, for better or

156

for worse, to the individual preference, of each parent or couple (within the acceptable parameters of each culture.)

Leaving each parent to direct their children in their own way makes less and less sense as our young people arrive in a New Age, where, as we have seen, experience counts much less than it once did. Of course, young people have *always* rejected some of their parents' advice, but what is different, and disturbing, now is that even when they accept it, they *do not benefit, because the advice is outdated.* We need better ways of parenting, more suitable for the Empowered young people of the New Age.

Many of our previously-accepted theories of human development were disrupted when, because of the Internet— and particularly You Tube—young people began to be aware of much more at far younger ages (although not necessarily in the "curricular areas" of school.) Because of this, the intellectual development of a huge percentage of our young people has soared, while their emotional development (without the same kinds of factors propelling it), remained the same. In fact, emotional development may even have slowed in some cases, though increased autism and bullying. The result was to disrupt whatever synchronicity we may previously have assumed, as guides, between intellectual and social development.

This same issue applies to the next "old" phase as well— Schooling (i.e., being a student.)

How *Schooling* Now Fails Our Young People

I presented and discussed a number of the reasons schooling now fails our young people in Chapter 7. High among them are schooling's academic nature (which, as we include more and more young people suits less and less of them), its lack of almost any real-world accomplishment (which young people crave), and its content being almost exclusively about the past, (which young people find increasingly irrelevant). While knowledge from the past can, as we know, be relevant, it is only *useful* when it is asked for. Schooling, as we saw earlier, *pushes things into young people,* rather than bringing unique things out of them. That is why more and more young people are rejecting the "schooling" we put them through. And schooling is a long phase, typically lasting many years.

The content of the "student" phase, unlike that of the parenting phase, is not left to each family. The content—and form—of that stage has become standardized, and pretty much the same, everywhere. Many relate this standardization to producing the workers we needed for an industrial economy. I believe it is also a result of colonialism.

But whatever the reasons, schooling has become very standard, worldwide. All children (if and when they go to school) first study reading, writing and arithmetic, and then math, local language, science, history and geography. (In the English-speaking world I call this standard curriculum *"THE MESS"*—*M*ath, *E*nglish, *S*cience, *S*ocial studies.)

The difference between schools is less a matter of *what* is put into young people, it is mostly a matter of *how*. Although some assert there are great differences between public, private, charter, and experimental schools, they all do the same thing—only marginally differently.

Standardization of schooling (and education) in the old frame also led to the idea that we could assess its "quality." The United Nations, in its SDG number 4, calls for a "quality" education for all. But defining and comparing quality of schools and education— necessary in the old frame—is a challenge.

PISA Doesn't Help

That challenge was taken up by the Organization for Economic Cooperation and Development, or OECD, who reasoned that since almost all young people around the world were (are) doing roughly the same thing in school, they could use a single test, given in every country, to compare young people and see where learning was being done the best. Their test, given to 15-year-olds, is called PISA (Program for International Student Assessment). PISA was given, initially, in a selection of schools in 52 countries. Most recently it has expanded to 79 out of the world's roughly 208 individual countries. Every three years, The OECD publishes tables ranking all these countries by average PISA scores. The countries' average scores show up in "size places" on a bar chart, much as teachers used to line up their pupils by grade ranking in class.

Having a higher PISA ranking became highly coveted by governments. When the rankings appear, politicians and educators from around the world rush to those countries at the top—e.g., Finland, Shanghai, Singapore—to closely observe the winners' methods and copy them. Thus, the scores became an incentive for some places to initiate various methods and reforms in order to generate higher PISA scores—just as OECD intended.

That sounds good—so why do I say it hasn't it helped? The reason is that while it may have helped the old frame of education in some ways, that frame is now ending. PISA does not help move us to the new frame of empowerment. All the PISA rankings *take place within the old frame of teaching the same things to everyone and having learning as the goal.* Despite OECD's ongoing efforts to add new skills such as problem solving to PISA, it is *the frame within which PISA takes place* that is no longer useful to young people, no matter how it is used or who may use it best.

How *Finding a Job* Now Fails Our Young People

Finally, the "job-finding" stage is also failing our young people, in big ways. Unemployment—especially youth unemployment—is huge in many places, despite in many cases, there being, numerically, enough jobs available for all. Many cite a lack of training as the reason, but there is still, as yet no global good way to universally connect what is needed by employers with workers who can (or potentially can) supply it. There are also few, if any ways to identify young peoples' unique individual skill sets and connect them to situations where they can be of use. So the job-finding stage almost universally left largely to chance and to whom you happen to know or be connected with, with countries deciding, for political reasons, who can (and can't) work where.

A New Growing-Up Frame for a New Age

The good news, as we enter the New Age of Empowerment, is that to deal with all these failures, a new and more empowering frame and process for growing up in this New Age is slowly emerging. There exists a new, empowering frame for growing up as a young person—anywhere—and a new frame for adults raising children and helping them grow up. As the acronym indicates, this new frame is 'FAR' more empowering than the previous one:

This new frame offers a "new taxonomy" for Growing Up Empowered":

The New Taxonomy for "GROWING UP EMPOWERED"

	Up to Now	New
Starting (Utero->~5)	HOME with parents (or substitutes) who control you & decide what is good/best for you. Only options are to welcome it, submit, or resist.	HOME+CLOUD w/parents & on own. You begin to gain self-knowledge of your beliefs, uniqueness, connections & powers, & discover what is best for you. You start to become Symbiotic w/ tech. Parents guide & curate. You can find additional parenting.
Expanding (~6->~20)	SCHOOL with educators. Their curriculum determines what is good for you. You have limited choices. Your task is learning whatever is presented. You do well, or poorly, or drop out.	EMPOWERMENT HUB with guides and coaches. You continually accomplish with Impact, following only your own interests. You have unlimited choices & create strong connections around the world. You find how and where you best add value. Everyone succeeds.
Realizing (Start time varies; stage lasts entire lifetime)	JOB FINDING & JOB DOING You flounder, using whatever connections you happen to have. You often choose what pays most, like it or not. Some get lucky, most don't.	CONTINUOUS VALUE-ADDING, with mentors, coaches and technology. You find what is best for you and do it, striving to realize your dreams and often doing so. You continually evolve, change and grow.

Dream Realization + Individual Development for All

What makes me think that this new frame and taxonomy are far better (i.e., more useful) than the ones from the past?

The first reason is that they are based on the universal wish and desire to *REALIZE ONE'S DREAMS*. In the old frame we may say these words to young people, but very seldom happens—particularly while they are young.

The second reason is that they are based on young people's *INDIVIDUAL UNIQUENESS*. The old frame is based only on average commonalities.

The third reason is that it offers new and *BETTER ROLES AND GOALS*—to both young people and to those raising them. It puts young people in the more empowered role of masters of their own destiny and makes their goal "being themselves" and using their empowerment to accomplish for the good of the world. It puts parents in the role of "curators" rather than "owners" of their children, with a goal to bring out their best aspects and accomplishments. It puts educators in the role of coaches and guides and changes their goals from producing "learning" (a means) but on producing accomplishments (a useful "end.") And for all, it offers the hopeful message that it is indeed possible to realize many of your dreams— and that that is worth striving for.

New Stages, New Expectations

The old growing-up frame was based, to a large extent, on outdated expectations and beliefs about what young people could do at fixed stages of human development—stages that applied to all—and what was needed at each stage. The old frame included specific beliefs about what young humans should be doing at each chronological age (on average within a range), as well as what they should be doing at each of the "old" stages of growing up (home, school, work). These old, 20th century beliefs about young people's development had gradually evolved over time—changing, for example, to fit the shift from an agricultural to an industrial age. They also differed, somewhat, in different places and cultures. But

162

overall, By the late 20th century, they became remarkably the same all over the world. The developmental theories of Jean Piaget, coupled with a global academic curriculum (influenced only somewhat by local traditions), came to dominate in the majority of places. It was generally accepted that *all* humans growing up went through—roughly at the same pace—specific stages in their physical development, emotional development, and intellectual development. Our job as adults in the old frame, therefore, was to direct our young people through the three stages of parenting, schooling, and job-finding.

Re-framing the Stages

I believe that in the New Age of Empowerment, the stages of growing up are changing to fit humans' changing culture and goals. The goal is no longer to produce cogs for the industrial age, but is now, I believe, *to produce good, empowered, people who will improve the world in the future.* I am therefore suggesting that in the New Age of Empowerment we re-frame and re-naming the growing up stages:

From Parenting, Schooling, and Job Finding,

To **Starting (Finding), Expanding (Applying), and Realizing.**

I suggest that such a new re-frame of "growing up" will be extremely helpful to young people—and to us all— today and in the future, in moving toward the new goal of producing good, empowered, world-improving people. All should derive optimism from re-framing each of the stages of growing up in this new way.

How Do We Make the Transition?

In the following chapters I will discuss in more detail the re-framing of each of the individual stages of the new, more empowering growing-up process.

I will do so in chronological order—starting from reframing the Starting/Finding phase (Parenting + the Basics), followed by the Expanding stage (The school years, Assessment, The new Empowerment Hub concept, and Higher education), and finally the Realizing stage (Meaningful work)—for the New Age of Empowerment.

As we do, please always keep in mind that

The new overall goal for young people in the 21st century is
TO GROW UP EMPOWERED.

and that

EMPOWERMENT IS SELF DIRECTION PLUS ACCOMPLISHMENT WITH IMPACT.

Harbingers

Not too long ago I had the good fortune of being contacted about my ideas by Leo Wölfel, a 20-year-old from in Munich, Germany, who was in the process of figuring out his 21st century life. It has since become a great friendship.

What I first noted, and liked, about Leo, is that he is a "seeker." He had, contrary to his parents' preference, dropped out after the German equivalent of High School, and was resisting enrolling in university—although still wondering if he should.

What Leo understood, profoundly, was that it was a different world he was going into, and that he had to find his own way. As he and I discussed options, he coined, to describe his preferred alternative, the term "Empowerment Hub", which I have now begun using and promoting around the world (See Chapter 14).

I see Leo's quest for a way that fits his uniqueness—rather than accepting and doing his best within the existing path—as a harbinger of what all young people will do in the future.

Leo has visited many schools and places in his quest, which is still ongoing. But he has never given up on his dreams. Nor, I hope, will he.

Reflection Question

Do *you* think the worlds' framework for growing up needs re-framing for the New Age of Empowerment? In what way(s)?

Now, let us look, in turn, at each of the stages of growing up, and the new ways I suggest re-framing them.

Chapter 14

RE-FRAMING PARENTING and BEING PARENTED FOR EMPOWERMENT

From {Ownership and Control
}
to [Curation and Empowerment]

HUMANS DON'T, AS YET, spring forth as fully grown and developed adults (although perhaps in the future they will.) But for now, every human is born helpless, not fully developed, and goes through an initial phase—between conception and roughly age 5— when they need to be cared for, in some way, by one or more adults. In the old frame, this is often called the "parenting" stage of growing up.

This parenting phase of development takes place primarily in whatever happens to be that child's home, with whatever family— or substitute— a child happens to have. Helping their children get started is usually seen as the job of those who have had the children—with the help of whatever additions and/or substitutes are available to help, such as extended family, community, or care centers.

There is no formula for parenting that consistently works. There are huge numbers of variables, and a great many theories and opinions about how to do it. How parenting is done varies widely from country to country, region to region, local community to local community, culture to culture, and even family to family. Cutting across regions are multiple "styles" of parenting: e.g., authoritarian, authoritative, permissive, indifferent, etc. [22] Results, of course, vary considerably. Some parents (or substitutes) seem to do a much better job than others.

Reframing Starting and Parenting

In reframing the parenting stage of growing up, my intention is not to review all these styles and theories. The question I pose, rather, is *whether the initial phase for all people under 5 years old can be more empowering than it currently is*. What kinds of parenting—and experiences of being parented—will most empower all young people in their New Age? Can we re-frame both "parenting" and the experience of "being parented" to maximally empower every young person who enters the world?

I believe we can.

The Old Frame: Ownership

Underneath all the cultures and styles of parenting, there lies, I believe one fundamental old frame: "ownership." The world's overall frame for parenting has been, up until now, that parents "own" their minor children—they are the "total boss" of them. In that frame, parents have almost complete power and control over their children up till a certain age. Outside of some limits of law— such as not being allowed to seriously physically abuse their children or kill them—parents can do with them as they like.

Ideally, "doing what they like with their children" means loving them and nurturing them. But in more situations than we would probably like to admit it also includes screaming at them, hitting them, punishing them, depriving them, and in extreme cases even enslaving and selling them. Hopefully it is clear that none of these last things—even the less extreme—are good or empowering for young people.

Yet ownership of children by their parents is a very old, and widely held frame. It is one that, I believe, appeals to many parents—partially, perhaps, because it *does* give them control over something in their life.

Parents Are Always Right

In this "ownership" frame, parents—almost no matter what they do or don't do—are always right. In many cases, the child cannot even express an opinion—and even when they can, if the parent disagrees they have no recourse. Nor does anyone else have a say: "Don't tell me how to raise my child" is an oft-heard phrase from parents in this frame.

Young people often start to resist this ownership frame very early on—about issues from feeding to bedtimes. Once they can talk, an oft-heard phrase from young people in this frame is "You are not the boss of me."

Sadly, in this old frame, they are.

Passing Down

A second element strongly characterizing the old frame is parents' insistence on passing down their own beliefs to their children. This passing-down happens both purposefully and to a large extent unconsciously. Parents talk to their babies and toddlers, dress them, include them in rituals like meals and religious services, tell them what to do and not to do, and in doing so pass their beliefs along to their children.

Much of this "belief-passing" happens in the starting phase of growing up. "Give me a child until the age of seven and I will show you the man," said Saint Augustine. Neuroscientists, in more recent times, have come to understand the importance of this time when the child starts to interact with the world and how those interactions shape the young peoples' neural connections. scientists still have much to learn, however, about the transfer of beliefs from parents.

The transfer of beliefs continues in the next expanding and applying phase of growing up as well, as parents—again with total control—send their child to schools of their choice.

Reframing the Relationship between Parents and Young Children to be More Empowering

Some might argue this ownership frame—and its transfer of beliefs—are actually empowering for young people. I believe it is the opposite. I believe we can re-frame the parenting stage of growing up to be far more empowering and useful to the young people of the New Age.

I suggest the needed re-framing, in its broadest outlines, is:

> *From parents as "owners" of their children, and always in control of them,*
>
> **To parents as "curators" of their children, whose role is to bring out the uniqueness, and the unique "value-add," of each child.**

Empowering one's children in this way—i.e., by helping each one find and develop their own uniqueness and unique "value-add," requires parents giving their children, at early ages, more self-knowledge, and more control—as well as an early start toward their new symbiosis with digital technology.

In the New Age of Empowerment, the growing-up process will still benefit greatly, I believe, from adult guidance. But making that process empowering requires a *new kind* of adult guidance, more akin to "curation" than ownership. (Note: I discuss the concept of "unique value-add" in Chapter 17.)

Requirements for an Empowering "Starting Phase": Respect, Trust, and Independence

Among the most important elements in making the starting phase or growing up a period of empowerment are Respect, Trust, and Independence. The more a parent gives these to a child, the more empowered the child will be. In her 2020 a book called *How to Raise Successful People,* [23] Esther Wojcicki, whose three daughters have all grown up to be extremely successful professionals, attributes her success at parenting to having given her children, from the earliest ages, as much Trust, Respect, and Independence as she possibly could—far more than most.

For Esther, respect is paramount. Even babies and toddlers have opinions, and respecting those opinions as real and important—and not just a place where you as an adult know better—is key to empowerment. Any *dis*respect, such as not admitting that the young person (at any age) may be right, is dis-empowering, whether it comes to feeding, where they can go, or anything else.

Also empowering for Esther is trusting your child—even in early years, and even though they will always push the limits. While it is a parent's job to as much as possible keep their kids from harm, being over-protective is disempowering. Another highly empowering thing parents can do is to give young people independence—and let them make mistakes. It is the parents who help children trust their own judgment as much as the parents' who are most strongly empowering their kids for the future.

Esther's approach to parenting—described in her book using the acronym "T.R.I.C.K." (Trust, Respect, independence Collaboration and Kindness)—is an extremely empowering one. I consider T.R.I.C.K. to be a "New Empowering Basic" for raising young people in the New Age.

Reframing All Young People as Having Goals

An important belief in the old parenting frame—one that definitely needs revising for the New Age of Empowerment—is that "young people don't know what they want." This belief needs a re-frame because it is just not true.

Adults often view very young people—babies—as helpless: They can't, initially, feed themselves, get around, or do almost anything physical except change position. But that doesn't mean they aren't thinking—or that they can't think. The truth is that even infants can, do, constantly. [24]

Nor is it true that young people—even infants—don't have goals. They absolutely do, at every minute. They may want food, they may want comfort, they may want to be hugged. And they express these goals—in ways that parents who want to empower them need to learn to interpret better. The most empowered young people are those who find, as early as possible, the connection between their actions and getting what they want and need—and the most empowering parents are the ones who give it to them.

A badly needed re-frame is:

> *From young people not having their own, specific goals,*
>
> **To young people all having very specific goals—and our job as parents being to understand & help satisfy them.**

That is what I mean by *curation*. Curation is bringing out the best in something, not shaping it to your own purposes. Curation is a process which, for maximum empowerment, needs to start in, and continue through, all the parenting years. The most empowering thing a child can get from its earliest years is the knowledge that it can have its own goals and find ways—and get help—in reaching them. This may seem like common sense, but it is amazing how often it is not the case.

As young people become older and more familiar with their world, their goals start to get bigger and longer-term. It is amazing to me how much parental energy is spent on tamping our young people's goals down and how many adults accept, at face value, a young person's assertion that they don't have any goals. One can almost always find them if one digs. Empowerment and curation require doing so.

A Parents' Manual for Empowerment

The old parenting frame of "ownership," suggests that there might be an "owner's manual"—something many new parents would dearly love to have. But no such manual, of course, exists. At different times in different places certain books (or folklore) have served that purpose—Esther Wojcicki's book is I think, a good one for our times. But there is no manual for human parenting that guarantees, if followed, that every child (and parent) will be successful.

So, what about a manual, or handbook, for empowerment? I.e., laying out steps to ensure every young person has an empowering parenting experience? Were I to write one I would start it by suggesting parents be be "caring, responsive adults" who begin by giving every child love, because love is perhaps the most empowering thing humans can give one another. Next would come sensitivity and careful listening to young people, necessary for empowerment because you can only help people—in ways they want to be helped—if you know what that is. (As many parents eventually find out, that may not be at all what you think—or what you wanted at their age.)

I will discuss new "empowerment basics" in the next chapter, but here are three areas to consider:

1. What Parents Pass Down

What beliefs, if any, should parents pass down to their children to empower them? Passing down our own beliefs to our children is a key aspect of the old parenting frame. Should it be part of the new frame as well? If so, what beliefs should we pass down to young people, from generation to generation, in order to empower them? This, too, needs a re-frame.

After all the millennia of human civilization, there are some beliefs that no one, I think, would argue about. "Do unto others as you would have them do unto to you." "Do not murder or steal." "Don't be false." These exist, with only slight variations, in almost all places and cultures. I strongly support passing these fundamental and helpful beliefs for society down to all young humans, as they are bases for all human cohesion—and being able to work with others is certainly empowering. But there are, I believe, very few of these—fewer in number than even the famous "Ten commandments."

And beyond those few, "passing-down" gets tricky. Should we pass down specific cultural practices? (Many are disempowering.) Religious ideas? (Ditto). Art and Literature? (Some is empowering and some isn't.) Historical knowledge? (Often empowering only to some.) Scientific knowledge? (Some would disagree about it.)

I think in that in terms of empowerment, passing down any of these things in a New Age of Empowerment is fraught.

2. Giving Young People Self-Knowledge

Yet every young person grows up with questions about themself.

> *What I believe is most empowering to pass on to young people is "how to obtain self-knowledge."*

Among the most empowering things that can come out of parenting, and first five years of life, are feelings of self-worth, self-confidence, and a sense—albeit an early one—of *who you are*. This includes your dreams, what you care about, what you are good at, and what you love to do. One might think that the first five years of life would automatically provide young people with a font of such knowledge and understanding about themselves that they could use to build a successful life. But that is far from universally the case.

> **In the old "ownership" frame, you turn out to be very much whom you are *told* you are.**

We have always known that the starting phase—roughly the first five years—is an important period for human development, but only recently are we learning, from scientists, more about *why* this period

174

is so important. Neurologically, it appears to be the time when the most lasting connections are formed in the brain, and the time when some of our deepest beliefs are formed about who we are. A developing human brain reacts deeply with the world around it, and development—and the adult we become—very much depends on one's early environment and experiences.

The environment one gets as a young person, however, is totally a matter of chance and the parents (or substitutes) the young person happens to have. But here is a useful and empowering goal, and re-frame, for parenting:

---

*From passing down what **you** think is important,*

To helping young people find out who THEY are, what they want, and how to get it.

---

3. Providing Empowering Beliefs

Growing up with empowering beliefs is one of the most important things to do. Beliefs, as we saw in Chapter 4, guide a person's whole life—and are not easy to change once formed, and can be either empowering or disempowering. Beliefs are, to a large extent instilled in people—very often by their parents—in the first years of life. It has always surprised (and disheartened) me that— since we have so much control over young people's beliefs—we don't give them beliefs that are more useful and empowering.

People are not born, for example, hating other groups, or with particular cultural strictures—those disempowering beliefs are instilled, mostly by parenting. Parents could, instead, be instilling far more useful and empowering beliefs in their children.

Many think that the religious beliefs they instill (if they do) are empowering. But here are my suggestions of beliefs that I believe are important for young people to hold in the Age of Empowerment that are ore more empowering, and that parents *could* instill. (Note: These are also published separately as a free online book, in multiple languages, at http://bit.ly/digital-natives-rising). A print version, entitled *DIGITAL NATIVES RISING* is also available.

- I am a member of the human race and a citizen of the world first—before my many other identities.

- I have a unique set of dreams, passions, strengths, and capabilities that no other human has.

- I can understand my uniqueness and apply it to bettering my world in my own way.

- I have the power to create positive change as an individual, and even more powerfully in teams.

- I can and will take my own dreams as seriously as I want to.

- My goal is to become a good, effective, world-improving person, doing the most good and the least harm I can.

- I will make my human and machine components work together well to solve problems…

- …and I will use my technology wisely for my own and others' good.

- I will strive to become my best self by combining what I care about most, what I am good at, and what I love to do.

- My key sources of happiness are LOVE, EMPATHY, GRATITUDE & OPTIMISM.

- I am entitled to TRUST, RESPECT, INDEPENDENCE, COLLABORATION & KINDNESS from others—and will give the same in return.

- I will build my self-esteem and self-confidence by continually accomplishing positive, useful, tasks in my community, country, and world...

- ... and will personally better my world by joining in world-improving projects.

- I will achieve my ideal life by balancing Socializing, exercise & play; Contributing to my world; and Renewing myself through food, sleep, and reflection.

- I am in charge of, and responsible for, my own life and future. I also welcome well-intentioned advice and guidance from all sources.

- I am free to believe whatever I want to. — But I am not free to cause harm to others or the world.

- I will not be under-respected, under-appreciated- or underestimated because of my age, gender— or anything else.

- I am nobody's pet, property, or slave. No person has the right to control me, beyond stopping me from doing harm.

- I know, and welcome, that my Digital Native life will be one of deep and continuous change.

- Because I know the beliefs I form growing up will control much of my life,

- I need to acquire all these 21st century beliefs that—no matter what any adult tells me—are right for me and my times.

My sense is that if every young person knew about, and followed these beliefs, it would be a far better world for everyone.

Are Children Pets?

An especially disempowering approach, often found in the old frame is treating your children as "pets." I imagine most parents, if asked if they do this, would answer, emphatically, no. But treating our young people as our pets is, in fact, a part of old frame that I have observed around the world, in a great variety of places, cultures and countries.

Just as with the animal pets adults own, adults often tell young people what to do, and where to go. They "potty train" them to go only where and when they say. (My son once had a teacher who wouldn't let him go to the bathroom before the class ended.) They make them "roll over" and perform whatever tricks have been taught to them—whenever we ask. (In the school years, the "performance of tricks" for adults' enjoyment is called "getting good grades on tests.") The phrase "teacher's pet" in English, is well-known. But compliance to our wishes (as we expect a pet to do) is not empowerment.

The needed re-frame is:

> From sometimes treating our young people as pets,
>
> **To always treating them as human beings who happen to be young, and who need to become empowered.**

Technology, Parenting and Empowerment

A big element increasing young people's power in the New Age is the arrival of technology and the Cloud. Digital technology—both devices and connectivity—is, today, a huge and controversial issue for parents of younger children. What is technology's role in the

178

new, empowered "Starting Phase" of growing up? When should those parents who can give children access to these new technologies? Are the new technologies harmful in the earliest years? Are they empowering?

Parents typically want to improve their children, and few leave this totally to chance. Early use of technologies has always given an edge to certain young people. Today medical technologies such as *in utero* operations, nutritional technologies, artificial organs and pumps, and now gene editing technologies are used—or tried —by many of the parents who can. While new technologies are often feared at first, introducing new technologies early in young people's lives has *always* been considered important by parents.

Parents use technology today to carry babies around safely, to strain and sterilize infants' food, to correct whatever birth defects we can, and (in some places) to straighten their teeth. Some parents use technology to play music *in utero* to their developing children in order to increase their capacities. (No one knows if this works, but there is plenty of technology to do it.)

Here are some additional thoughts about re-framing parenting and technology for empowerment:

Reading As an Expiring Technology

Writing down our thoughts, and later reading them, is one of human's greatest technologies (although often largely no longer thought of as such.) Those are the technologies for storage and retrieval of information that replaced, to a large extent human memory. Socrates, according to lore, was not happy about this— but Plato, his student, was. As a smart young person of his time, Plato moved quickly to adopt these technologies, and as a result, we still know of Socrates and his thinking.

Today almost all parents want their children to read, and most adults would see it as *dis*empowering *not* to teach a child to do so. But our technology is, again, profoundly changing. As we will see in the next chapter, modern technology makes storage and retrieval of information (which writing and reading are technologies for) something one can do through other means, including our voice (via recording and voice to text) and ears (via text to voice).

How much should parents encourage this shift in their children? Lest you think this is a silly question—who could possibly be against teaching all kids reading—I beg you to think of what things would be like if, when the techniques of writing down music were invented, we all just learned to read scores in our heads and stopped listening. In some sense we have done the same with Shakespeare and with poetry, for example, where the reading has, in a great many cases, supplanted the seen or heard. Not everyone would say this is positive.

Audio

We have reached a point with both audio and video technologies where they can begin to serve as primary means, in many cases. How can parents use this to further empower their children in the "Starting Phase" of growing up in the New Age of Empowerment?

We know, for example, that the sound of their own parents' voice is important to a child, and that a parent's talking to their child is a key to the child's development. Many have heard of a so-called millions of words gap between children from wealthy and poor families. Yet few parents can be with their children all the time.

So here's a re-framing question: What effect would the *continuous sound of a parents' particular voice* in their children's ears have on a young child's development? We don't actually know, but today's technologies can provide this opportunity—our young people in many places already constantly listen to music, often through earbuds. I have yet to see many studies on the long-term development effect this has had, other than on their hearing, but it certainly differentiates today's young people from those of the past.

Were a constant channel of the parent's voice available, (e.g., through recordings or chatbots) would younger children choose to have their parents' voice constantly in their ears when the parent wasn't there, just as they often choose to do with music? What should be on such a stream? If given the option, would they choose a different voice from that of a parent?

Which do you think would be better for a child's development: (1) having technology that speaks—in whatever voice the child finds comforting (including their parents')—whatever they want to hear, as many times as they want, on demand, , or (2) hearing the words of their nanny as she talks to her friends on the phone while she pushes their stroller—as I have seen a great many do in the streets of New York? When listening to the Harry Potter books, would Stephen Frye's or Jim Dale's voice be preferred to that of that of a parent if it were easy to swap the parent's voice in? I don't know, but technology is very close to being able to put a parent's voice into their children's ears constantly from birth. Very soon there will be an interactive "parent chatbot"—like today's Siri or Alexa—using the parent's voice. Will that be a good thing?

What About Game Technologies?: Re-framing Video Games As "Symbiosis Trainers"

One of the biggest challenges of the next 20 years, as I noted, is to help young people become symbiotic with technology as quickly as possible. Symbiosis is necessary so they can perform the tasks and address the problems of their times. My sense is that this symbiosis is best started as early as possible. That is part of the environment of the future. Why would any parent think they can successfully raise a child for the future by keeping them in an environment of the past?

This question become acute when it comes to videogames. Should a parent encourage their child to play, not care, or oppose it? I have, in the past, been very supportive of kids' playing videogames, as they are, a way to help young people become more symbiotic with technology—to make it into a part of them. Young people know this, and that is a big part of their attraction. Their fast-moving parts and interactions, demand a new form of symbiosis. I will never forget the voice of the high-school girl saying, when asked l if she played videogames. "No, my parents deprived me." Recently, the old game of Tetris has returned to popularity with a new generation of players who play in a far more symbiotic manner, amazing the players of the past.

But videogames are also a huge money-maker for some adults. As like anything else that offers big financial gains, humans are willing to make all kinds of moral adjustments in order to get it. The companies that make videogames work hard to make them as attractive as possible. Some critics claim makers are "addicting our kids" to the games through deliberately pernicious "dopamine hits." I don't buy the deliberate addiction argument. Giving people excitement—and the concomitant brain chemicals that accompany it—is the goal in a great many domains. Addiction, however, very much depends on the individual young person— there are a small number with "addictive personalities" who are better off avoiding a great many things, probably including videogames. But I see the games more as training young people to work more symbiotically with the new machine systems. It is game players, for example, who are chosen to program and pilot the new flights of drones—civilian and military, in symbiosis with artificial intelligence. In some cases, it can help make them better robotic surgeons.

A complaint I do have with the game makers is that they often exploit young people financially, making them feel they need all sorts of useless-outside-the-game add ons, which cost real money. Parents should be on guard against this. But overall, think this fear of videogames is not justified. I once heard a very successful game designer, who had grown up constantly playing videogames say— only half-jokingly, and with a big smile—"I was raised by machine." I'm certainly not suggesting we let this happen *instead* of live parents, but this guy, at least, came out fine.

Using Young Peoples' Time "Wisely"?

The other issue is time. It is of course the case that game playing uses up children's time that could be spent on other activities. And a great many adults have their own ideas of what those activities should be. Some societies can limit game-playing time by decree: China's recently (as I write) passed laws to do this. Many parents, from the 20th century are torn—as I am when I hear my 16-year-old in his room having the some of best times in his life playing games with his friends and knowing that he prefers that over many other pastimes that I, as a 20th century parent might prefer for him— particularly school. But I do know he is empowering himself in the process, and the in the world he is going into, not being able to interact symbiotically with technology will be a handicap.

I think the most useful re-frame here for parents is this:

> *From video gaming being a waste of young peoples' time,*
>
> **To video gaming being excellent preparation for symbiosis.**

To What End?

We are still left, however, with the question of "to what end" the symbiosis will be put. Here our overall parenting re-frame—from direction to curation—is again useful, because

> **While play feels good, it does not feel as good as accomplishing something you feel improves your world.**

While I think it is *not at all* useful to young people to *prevent* them playing games they enjoy, I think it is part of the new parenting role of "curation" in the New Age of Empowerment, to help their children discover the most empowering uses of their time. Game playing can, in many instances be empowering far beyond just the symbiosis—some young people will become professionals, and there are so-called "serious games" that do social good—but it is not necessarily the case. My recommendation for parents has always been to watch and know your child.

Will Pre-School Help?

Many today think we can, and should, add some useful consistency to a child's early development by moving young people out of the parent-dominated stage earlier, through "pre-school." Whether that is a good idea, I think, depends very much on the nature of the pre-school experience—i.e., on whether or not that experience is controlling or empowering.

The issue in creating a standard, pre-school curriculum for the New Age of Empowerment is the same one as creating a "parenting manual":

> *every human is unique and different. And we are now in an age that needs to acknowledge that and build on it.*

I have always liked the metaphor of Brazilian author Rubem Alves, that schools can be either "cages" or "wings" for young people. (And, I would add, for their parents.) What works for some young people may not work for others—both schools, and parents, can, in some cases, actually harm young people. In general,

> *Those pre-schools (and parents) who standardize and control young people are cages. Those that act as wings are empowering.*

A final thing to say about pre-school and empowerment is that young people at that age (and, in fact, all ages) are a lot more capable that is often thought by adults—even without technology. Even three-year-olds can do projects with Measurable Positive Impact on their world—see https://youtu.be/5u1cCbSYh2Q for an inspiring example. So to be empowering for preschoolers in the New Age of Empowerment, preschool needs to include as many of these kinds of projects as possible.

Sorting and Matching

An issue related to empowerment that technology turns out to be really useful for—and good at—is matching and sorting. This is, today, the basis for all commercial "recommendation engines" including retail apps like Amazon and dating apps like eHarmony and Tinder. Although there may be downsides, it can be very empowering to be able to quickly and easily find exactly the match you need. And this is what is happening—a growing number of people—especially young people— are finding good matches—and even mates—online through these methods.

Sorting and matching of people is by no means new. In some cultures, children are observed very early to see if they exhibit special talents (often physical aptitudes for certain sports or in some cases intellectual prowess.) If so, they are sent off to be brought up and "parented" in particular ways—over which, they, and even their biological parents, have little control. Military organizations have always done this to be better. Religions often do this as well. In some places and cultures, and at some levels (e.g., ruling families) there are professional and political match makers, often starting at birth.

Most parents, however, are left to do much of the sorting and matching job for their children on their own. Choosing matches for your child—whether it be toys, friends, pre-schools, or public or private schools—is typically left to parental judgment and available options, cost concerns, etc. Can we do better? I believe so, and technology can help in a major way.

A Future Re-frame: Parenting You Choose?

Although at this point this is speculative, one way this could be done is by using technology to connect children, earlier in life, with the kinds of parenting they need. This does not have to replace biological parents, it can supplement them, and their children with additional parenting opportunities. Our new technology—as it matures—can help connect young people—letting them choose, if not their actual parents, at least their additional ones.

This not a new idea—there have been, and still are, cultures where parenting of the youngest is far more widespread and shared. I am not suggesting that every 1–5-year-old—or their parents— can—or should—do this. Nor do I think that we should *compel* anyone—parent or child—to do it. But it could be helpful.

In the New Age, when Empowerment is what counts, the set of parents one happens to get through birth is likely no longer to be empowering enough for *any* child—and can potentially be positively supplemented—with technology—for all. There is, of course, be a dystopian version of this, i.e., "indoctrination" of young people, which is what some see happening through social media, but I think that is a danger we can avoid. Rather, I believe we will invent ways, certainly in the next 20 years, to get more extended parenting that is empowering and useful. This will come not just as in the past from grandparents or others who are related, but from all adults who have specific things to offer that would benefit each young person, starting even from a very early age. As young people acquire more self-knowledge, I hope we will be able to provide extended parent-matching based on it and, in a positive loop, extend it further.

So, another parenting re-frame I believe is empowering in the New Age is:

From every person having only the parents they get,

To every person who happens to be young also being matched with a supplementary "parenting" process that will maximally benefit them.

Some may think this is what "pre-school" and "school" already is and does. But I know we can go much further in this area, to everyone's benefit. And it can begin in the earliest years. A new vision of a more empowering "pre-school" —not as a "school" but as an empowering experience—would be a positive step in this direction.

Getting the Most Empowerment out of Being Parented

Finally, it is important to also re-frame the starting phase of growing up through the lenses on the other side—i.e., from the young people's perspective. How do they see being parented, and is there a more empowering frame for them?

Even though they are much affected by parenting, it is rarely thought that young people have much influence on how they are parented. Can they, to their benefit, have more in the New Age of Empowerment? Can we re-frame parenting *from the young person's perspective* (i.e., "being parented") so that young people in the New Age of Empowerment get the most out of it (both as "starters" and as they get older)? One way we can re-frame empowering parenting, from the young person's perspective, is as "Getting the Ultimate Gift."

The Ultimate Gift for Young People

In my view, beyond being truly loved, the best and most empowering gift a young person can ever get is:

finding an adult who sees you for who ***you think you are,*** and who gives you guidance that helps you get to ***where you want to go.***

In the best of cases this gift come from your parents, but it very often does not.

Heretofore, young people had very few ways to find this ultimate gift by themselves—it was almost entirely a matter of chance. I believe that in the New Age of Empowerment they will have far more power and influence in this area. Here is a useful re-frame for most people who happen to be young:

> *From having <u>only</u> the parents you get by chance,*
>
> **To being able to choose your own by finding mentors, and alternative parenting, if necessary, that suit you better. And thus, in a sense, to being "parented by the world."**

I cannot say exactly how this will happen—it is a re-framing mechanism that needs to be invented over the next 20 years. But I do hope people—young and old—will be open to this kind of experimentation. The randomness of one's parents—along with the randomness of the teachers one gets, is, in my view, too important not to be addressed and modified, somehow, in the New Age of Empowerment.

Bottom Line for the New Starting/Parenting Stage of Growing Up

We are moving, generationally, from a time of ownership and control of children by their parents to a time of empowerment of young people by themselves and by society. The most empowering things that can come out of the starting and parenting phase of life are love, self-knowledge, self-confidence, and self-esteem, coupled with the knowledge that there are adults who not only want to help you find these things—*from your point of view*—but really *can* help you find them and apply them to real-world accomplishments whose impact you can point to and of which you can be proud.

To get there, we need to re-frame the relationship between parents and young children in ways that are much more empowering to the young. We need to recognize that it is *their* dreams, *their* goals and *their* unique value-add that we are supporting and that it is our job, as parents to curate. And, perhaps hardest of all, it means we must accept that the beliefs they acquire and live by, and the new symbiosis they achieve with technology in the New Age of Empowerment while positive for them—may not be our own.

Harbingers

As a harbinger of parents who have already begun the new "starting phase" of the New Age of Empowerment I will cite Georgina Guerra, the mother of the girl in Mexico (also named Georgina) who we saw start a successful project during Covid time. Here is the story the mother told me: "When my daughter was home from school on quarantine with little to do, I handed her a big piece of blank paper saying: 'Put down your dream and your vision for these times.' The result was the highly successful project of creating distributing "kits" described earlier.

What if instead of running around trying to get their children into "remote learning" as so many parents did during Covid time—more parents had taken this alternative approach with their children. What new things would it have produced? Parents, by the way, can still do this.

Father Gerry Aab, in South Africa encouraged his daughter, Alexa, to participate in an Empowerment Hub called *Planet Pilots*. (More on those in Chapter 15.) When asked why she liked it, Alexa commented "That is where I can be myself." Is that not something for parents to encourage?

Reflection Questions

How were you parented? Did you feel empowered or disempowered? Were your parents the ones you would have chosen, or would you have liked to have additional ones? How might you parent differently now? Do you think your children will want to parent differently than you? (Ask them!)

Do you agree that our young people are often "not themselves" in our world? If not, *who are* the young people in the world in most of the places they go? Do they need to create new places of own? Can we help?

Do we need, in our new parental role of curation rather than direction, to re-frame new "basics" for our children in the New Age of Empowerment.

I believe we do, and what these new, more empowering "basics" are the subject of the next chapter.

Chapter 15

RE-FRAMING 'THE BASICS' FOR THE NEW AGE OF EMPOWERMENT

From {The old artifacts of Reading, Writing and Calculating}
to [Preparation for Meeting the New Needs]

EVERY PARENT WILL TELL YOU, rightly, that they want their children to acquire, as early as possible, "the basics"—i.e., the things that are "absolutely necessary" for future success.

Up until recently, we generally thought we knew what those were. But I suggest "the basics" for young people are now changing—rapidly—and particularly with our 20-year time horizon in mind.

What "basics" will today's young people need to empower them for the mid-to-late 21st century—the New Age of Empowerment? That will surely be a world of far more accomplishment and impact by young people. In the previous chapter we looked at some things that parents can do to empower their children in the new starting phase of growing up. As they move into the next phase of expanding and applying are there "new basics" for every young person to now begin to acquire and use during that time?

In this expanding/applying phase young people will likely move—as we will see in the coming chapters—from today's education to projects, from academic schools to Empowerment Hubs, and from finding jobs to "adding value." Are the necessary basics for this still the same ones as before? Or do what are now known as "the basics" need re-framing?

By now you know my answer.

The Old Basics of Reading Writing and Arithmetic Are from an Old Frame

Most still think of as "The Basics" what are called, in some places, the old "3 R's": Reading, wRiting and aRithmetic (i.e., calculation by hand). Those are certainly the basics of the old frame of academic learning. Without them, in that old frame, you are severely handicapped—and often seen as a lesser person in the world. In that old frame everyone, without exception, needs them. That is why we try so hard today—although not always effectively—to extend those skills to all.

Storage, Retrieval and Sharing of Ideas: Writing and Reading

Storage, retrieval and sharing of ideas and information are fundamental to human society and advancement— I don't know anyone who would argue that they are not important. They are also fundamental to empowerment.

In the last several centuries, humans have gotten very used to, and comfortable with certain very successful ways of doing these things. Today, if you dare ask: "Are reading writing and arithmetic still the basics all young people need to succeed in the mid-to-late 21st century future?"—as I do—you will typically be met—as I often am—with stiff resistance.

193

I would note, though, that reading, writing and hand calculation are very difficult skills for many to learn. They are not, at all, like speaking, which comes naturally to humans. Teaching these things—now seen as "basics"—requires required a huge corps of human teachers throughout the world. Today, of course, many are experimenting with new, technology-based ways of teaching these skills to all young people—but still without leaving the old academic frame.

Because these particular "basics" are so ingrained and prized in most cultures in the world, few who were raised in the 20th century will say they are no longer basic or needed. It is, I have found, very hard to get people to re-frame in this area. But I will try.

Symbiosis Makes Things Different

The question I ask is "Are those old basics of reading, writing and arithmetic —although clearly still useful today—outdated for a New Age of Empowerment as methods for storage, retrieval and sharing of information?"

We all know our necessary personal knowledge, as individuals, changes as humans advance. We no longer need to all know how to fish, or hunt, or build our own houses, or make our own clothes— all once "basics" for survival. Methods, too, change. No one today would use cuneiform or chiseled blocks to store and retrieve information—except possibly on gravestones—yet they were once the most advanced methods humans had for doing this. For millennia after they were invented, reading and writing were not considered basic for all—they were the privileged methods of only a few. It is only in the last century that most humans moved to text literacy. That coincides, of course, with the time when all today's adults grew up.

Now, as the New Age of Empowerment begins. we are moving on again to new methods for storge, retrieval and communication of information. (And for calculation, which I will discuss in a minute.)

A big re-frame we need regarding reading and writing is:

From seeing reading and writing as basic human needs.

To seeing "storing and retrieving information" as the basic human need—and to always doing so in symbiosis with the current best technology.

For quite a while that current "best technology" has been reading and writing of printed text. This has been the most efficient way to store and retrieve information for most humans for the last several hundred years of human history. But bear in mind that while "a few hundred years" may be a long time in an individual human's memory, it is but a blip in historical terms. Text—as useful as it has been in our times—is in a great many ways extremely inefficient. We have entered into a period where the best methods are changing quickly.

While text will never go away, it is unlikely to be the dominant method in 20 years that it is today. Because text is so ingrained, the shift away from it is hard for many 20th-century-raised adults to understand, or swallow. But it is important that our young people be prepared for this. In order for our young people to move successfully into their empowered future, I believe we need to re-frame what is "basic" for them in this area in the following way:

> *From needing to spend the years of effort needed to learn to read and write text in order to retrieve, store and share information,*
>
> **To moving more quickly to whatever method works best for each person—voice, hearing, visuals or means to be invented.**

What humans have stored over time is in many cases useful and is unlikely to be lost. But rather than continuing to force our old processes on our young people, we should instead be working to make access to everything humans have done far easier and more efficient for them.

How Necessary *ARE* Reading and Writing? — Why NOT Being Able to Read or Write is No Longer the Same Handicap

There is no question that reading and writing are useful skills to have today. But the situation is already changing rapidly for tomorrow. Communication will remain basic for humans, but how it is done is already quickly evolving. Like it or not, the age of "text primacy" is already on its way out. Already today—outside of certain relatively small circles—people rarely read many books, particularly after school forces them to. The number of people getting the bulk of their information—or entertainment—from text is seriously declining.

In the past—even in the 20th century—were I to have moved to a different country where I neither read nor write the language— China, for example, from the U.S.—I would have been totally cut off from communicating in that place and culture, unless and until I put in huge amounts of difficult study. But today, without any studying, I would be handicapped *only by my speed in using my mobile phone* to do those things in Chinese. Using my current smartphone—now seemingly advanced, but soon to be primitive—everything I might need that is written or spoken in Chinese could go directly into my ears—in English, my native language. I could write in Chinese by just speaking English into my phone. Those capabilities exist, very close to seamlessly, on my smartphone today. Using it would not be a problem, since much of China's digital infrastructure, hardware and software is at par with the best in the world.

In 20 Years

Now imagine what it will be like for today's young people in 20 years, which is the timeframe we are talking about—or even 5-10? It will be almost perfect. Nuances between languages that still exist will be overcome by the technology—just as they are today by the best human translators. And while today's availability and coverage is still spotty, it won't be in 20 years, when today's young people are adults.

Even so-called "texting" is already full of emojis, pictures, stickers, and acronyms. And while young peoples' thumbs have in many cases become able to enter text fast, anything can also be entered via voice (and retrieved that way as well.)

Not Disappear, but Become a Niche

I'm *not* saying—and I don't believe—that reading and writing will ever disappear. They almost certainly will not, as little ever does completely. But I believe that by the late 21st century, when today's young people are adults, reading and writing will no longer be as primary, or "basic" as they are today. By the mid-to-late 21st century neither reading or writing will be the "absolute necessities" they were in the 20th century—and still are for the moment. Rather, reading and writing, will be more like Latin and Greek are today in America—*artifacts*. Some people can still read and write those languages, and we do still regularly use certain Latin and Greek words and phrases. But today those languages are only specialties for a self-selected few. And anyone who *wants* to learn them can do so on the Web. So it will be, I believe, with reading and writing of all languages—though not, of course, for speaking.

This does **not** mean, importantly, that a person who wants to self-educate themselves through existing texts—, i.e., books—as many have famously done in the past—can no longer do so. In fact, today, doing so is far easier—every word those self-educators ever read can be heard through your ears as you walk down the street.

What Should We Do?

I believe it is reasonable to say that *"we should continue to teach reading and writing until other options are widely available to all."* But that is not what many adults say, or think. Most of the 20th century adults I talk to think reading and writing are useful skills *for all time*. But that ongoing usefulness is true *only for communication*—*not* for reading and writing. In fact, today—in a time when almost anything any person might once have done in reading and writing can be done in other forms—those former "basics" are often *great barriers* to people's full participation in the world.

What About Knowing How to Do Arithmetic Calculations by Hand? Is that still a "Basic"?

Let us now take arithmetic and simple numerical calculation by hand. Is that still a basic in the New Age of Empowerment? I believe this former "basic" needs a re-frame for the New Age as well.

Numbers are, of course, a great human invention/discovery. They are used and useful, almost universally, for describing certain many things, particularly patterns. Patterns are a fundamental part of nature, and mathematics is an important language for describing and expressing them. Every young person should know something about numbers—particularly things that may not be intuitive.

But hand calculation as a basic has passed. The needed re-frame for such arithmetical calculation is

---

From the importance of knowing how to calculate by hand,

To the importance of recognizing a numerical problem, having an intuitive sense of the answer, and when an exact answer is needed using our using our symbiotic technology parts to get it.

This is true not only for arithmetic, but for all mathematics including the most complex. For life in a time where almost everyone will have access to a calculator *as a symbiotic part of their body*, it no longer makes any sense to teach every young person to do arithmetical calculations by hand—any more than it still makes sense to memorize log tables or advanced multiplication tables—those were abandoned decades ago as better means became available.

So, WHAT IS Basic in the New Age of Empowerment?

If reading, writing, and arithmetic are no longer the basics they were in the 20th century, *what are* the "basics" for the New Age of Empowerment?

The most honest answer is that we don't completely know yet. We are, today, still in a transition phase of figuring out what the world, and its basics will be in the mid-to-late 21st century and beyond. Because things are now changing so fast, what comprises "the basics" may *always* remain in a transition phase, and never reach a new steady state lasting for centuries—as the previous group did. But I do believe we can make some good guesses for the mid-to-late 21st century—which is what we need now.

My Take

Communication—through speech and new means—will certainly remain basic. The numerical skills I just described will also still be important.

But the lists of so-called "21st century skills" that many have put out are, to me, more suspect. They are, really, just a re-emphasis of certain useful skills from the past. They are not bad to have, and may even help in some ways. But trying to teach any of them *in advance as "basics"* is not—as we have seen—the most useful approach.

The Basic Elements of Empowerment

There are four "basic" elements that I believe are needed for empowerment—all of which I have discussed previously in the book:

> - New, Empowering *BELIEFS*
> - Real-World *ACCOMPLISHMENT*
> - Technology & Team *SYMBIOSIS*
> - Self-knowledge and applied *UNIQUENESS*

Additionally, here is my current re-framing of additional basics needed in and for the New Age of Empowerment:

> *From reading, writing and arithmetic,*
>
> ***To a new combination of***
> **– "THE ACCOMPLISHMENT (ABCD) LOOP,"**
> **– "T.R.I.C.K.,"**
> **– ADAPTATION TO CONTINUOUS CHANGE, and**
> **– "L.E.G.O."**

This is what I mean by these:

THE ACCOMPLISHMENT ("ABCD") LOOP = is continuous iteration, via successive real world-impacting projects, of Accomplishing—Bettering Your World—Considering how you could do an even better job, and—Doing it again." This iterative loop is the primary means to Empowerment and to Accomplishment with Impact. Every young person should be doing this, at every age, continuously.

T.R.I.C.K. = is an acronym for Trust, Respect, Independence, Collaboration, and Kindness. These behaviors, first listed in this way by Esther Wojcicki, all lead to Empowerment. Every person young-or old—should give and receive Trust, Respect Independence, Collaboration, and Kindness continuously.

ADAPTATION TO CONTINUOUS CHANGE. In a continuously fast-evolving world, the best means to Empowerment will almost certainly change—most likely frequently. Every person should anticipate the need to change their current means and start using new ones—and become good at making these transitions as quickly and painlessly as possible.

L.E.G.O. = This is my personal acronym for Love, Empathy, Gratitude and Optimism. Every human needs these basic things to thrive. (This is different from the trademarked word (without the periods) which is not a basic need, but only a brand to sell more toys.)

"New Basics" for the New Age of Empowerment

Master **THE ACCOMPLISHMENT LOOP** **A**ccomplish useful things **D**o it again **B**etter Your World **C**onsider how to improve the process	Give and expect **T.R.I.C.K.** Trust, Respect, Independence, Collaboration, Kindness *Esther Wojcicki*
Be ready for **CONTINUOUS CHANGE**	Build up your **L.E.G.O.** Love, Empathy, Gratitude, Optimism

---

All four of these things, I believe, are basics for the New Age of Empowerment. But even with the others, they are only the start. They are basics: not enough—alone—for successful empowerment in the New Age, but very much helping form the right foundation.

From Where Will They Come?

How, and from where, should and will these "basics" come to young people? I believe they can all, and should all, begin with the starting phase of growing up—parenting—particularly with parents giving their children empowering beliefs. The acquisition of these basics should continue throughout the expanding/applying phase of growing up—primarily through the accomplishment (by young people) and coaching (by adults) of projects.

Replacing Our Current School Phase

But it is unlikely these new basics—and thus empowerment— will be acquired by young people if all we do is conceive of that expanding/applying phase as a continuation of 20th century academic "school." This is true, I believe, no matter how early we start (e.g., with pre-school.) School, as it is now conceived, all over the world, is *dis-empowering* for most young people. This is true *despite* all efforts—often herculean—on the part of teachers and administrators.

School, as we are about to see in the following Chapter, is just not the right solution for the New Age of Empowerment. Whether "reformed" or "enhanced with technology" it will not help young people move more easily into the New Age. But as we shall also see, there are new and better alternatives emerging to take school's place.

Harbingers

Harbingers of the "new basics" include all the young people in the world with mobile phones. Most see their devices as so basic to their existence as Symbiotic Empowered Hybrids that they fight—often fiercely—to prevent their being taken away from them. They know they are preparing themselves for symbiosis, in the only ways they currently can.

There are a few adult harbingers as well, in the new basics realm. One is Conrad Wolfram in the UK, who is on a mission to bring mathematics into the 21st century by requiring that all children to use computers to do it. His company, Mathematica, designed a math course (for Estonia) that begins with the frequently asked student question "Am I normal?" Wolfram's new kind of math can, and should, begin in Grade 1.

Another adult harbinger is Esther Wojcicki, whose acronym T.R.I.C.K. we just encountered as a new basic. Throughout her 40 years of teaching, Esther always struggled to get other teachers to see young people in the ways she did. Hopefully, her time is now quickly coming.

Reflection Question

Can you take a longer-term perspective on what the basics are for the people of tomorrow?

Now, with our new basics in hand, let's go re-frame our outdated "school years" and curricula.

Chapter 16

RE-FRAMING THE THE 'SCHOOL YEARS' AND CURRICULA FOR THE NEW AGE OF EMPOWERMENT

From {Learning}
To [Expanding by Accomplishing]

From {Classes}
To [Real-World-Impacting Projects]

From {Sequential Topics}
To [Sequential Accomplishments]

and

From {Schools}
To [Empowerment Hubs]

TODAY, IN MANY PLACES, we frame the years from roughly ages 6 to 21 as "the school years"—because school is the main activity young people are doing (or what adults would like them to be doing) during that time. In many places the law requires young people to be in school during some of those years. Yet increasingly, a great many young people resist, knowing that school, too often, *dis*-empowers them.

Can we re-frame these many years—which can comprise ten percent or more of many people's lives—to make them more useful and empowering for the future? I believe we can—and, if our goal is to truly help our young people—we must.

To begin, I suggest the following re-frame (and re-name) for those years, in the context of continually building Empowerment:

From the "school years,"

To the "Years of Expanding and Applying."

"Expanding": An Outpouring of Energy

Why do I call these years, from roughly 5-20, the "years of expanding"? It is not just because there is great physical growth during those years. Nor is it because "expansion," is confined only to those years. For humans, expansion (in a great many senses) begins in the womb and continues, ideally all one's life. There is certainly much expanding during the first five years of life.

But in the next period of growing up, from ages roughly 6-21, young people expand in many new senses. They become more aware of their own capabilities and of the world. They form longer-term goals. During this time, they actively extend themselves far beyond where they started in directions they want to go—which hopefully include bettering their world.

Interestingly and powerfully—although often confusingly—this expanding period also coincides with human sexual maturing and the drive to reproduce. The two are strongly linked, yet they often come into conflict in the education world, and are rarely discussed together. They ought to be, because

> **what comes from the expanding phase is a huge outpouring of energy, now largely unused for the benefit of all.**

This energy, both exploratory and sexual is today mostly tamped down by adults, who often try very hard to do so. *But it could be used*—and used far better than now. A better way of re-framing those expanding years is:

> *From years of tamping young people's energy down while putting information into their heads—and leaving them to them to explore physical changes on their own,*
>
> **To years of <u>utilizing all this energy</u> by encouraging dreams and accomplishments by all young people."**

How can we best do this?

Re-framing the Expanding/Applying Phase of Growing Up from education to Dreams and Accomplishments

In the world of the 20th century, the expanding/applying phase of growing up was called, in most places, "Getting an Education." The formal part of this education, which happened in schools, consisted of trying to put things into young people's heads. This included information that they couldn't easily find on their own and subjects that they might not encounter unless compelled to. The hope, and ideal was that doing so would open up young peoples' eyes to a larger world and stimulate new desires in them.

It was, in many ways a huge success story. Large numbers of people around the world benefitted from 20th century education—including me, and probably you as well. We should gratefully acknowledge the work of those that made it happen—those who worked in education in the 20th century deserve our profound thanks.

And because of education's success by the end of the 20th century, the world's adults—all raised in that century— saw its universal spread as a key goal. The United Nations adopted as its Fourth Sustainable Development Goal (SDG) "giving a 'quality education' to all."

Doubts—and The Need for a New Success Story

Yet even as far back as the mid-20th century, when the historian Will Durant designated education, as one of the "Peaks of Human Progress," [25] he wondered how permanent it would be. Durant's concern was valid, but not for the reason he thought. Durant feared—as many still do—that without "education" humanity would fall back into ignorance—as happened during the European Middle Ages. What Durant didn't foresee, however, is that education would be *supplanted*—because of a rise of new capabilities and beliefs within humans.

Capabilities, Dreams, and Accomplishments

We have discussed these new capabilities in previous chapters. Now, during the expanding/applying phase of growing up (ages 6-21) young people are getting to know them better, as they dream about possibilities and the future. Calling someone a "dreamer," in the past, was not always seen as positive, but in the New Age of Empowerment it needs to be, because:

> **The most useful thing we can do for young people as they expand during this period is help them focus on their dreams, and help them see—to the extent we can—what they could be doing and becoming in their future world.**

Going Beyond Education

So, even though education was a hugely successful strategy for the years between 6 and 12 *in the context of the 20th century*, that stage is now in need of serious updating and re-framing for the 21st century and the New Age of Empowerment.

The reason the expanding/applying phase needs a re-frame away from education is

> **the addition of huge new capabilities and connections for young people, accompanied by major belief changes.**

Those are things that education was not designed to address (and is not, I believe, capable of addressing).

Applying Your Uniqueness to the World

The New Age of Empowerment requires a shift

> *From "educated people"*
>
> **To "Empowered People."**

and to produce them we need to move:

> *From a system of learning in advance in classes and courses,*
>
> **To a new system of applying our own uniqueness to the world, through continuous accomplishment with Impact.**

The needed re-frame for the expanding/applying phase of growing up (roughly years 6-21) is, therefore,

> *From getting an education (i.e., from spending years studying and learning),*
>
> **To expanding and applying through realizing your dreams via continuous accomplishment of useful, real-world projects in areas that interest you.**

Where, and At What Levels?

This re-framing, and shift, will happen, I predict, at all levels, i.e., primary, middle, high-school, and college/university—starting as an alternative choice. Some of it will no doubt happen in existing schools, or school buildings.

Today, those existing buildings today serve the dual purpose of keeping young people safe while their parents work and teaching a curriculum. But as the needs of the world rapidly change from "educated people" to "empowered people," some will change—but only some schools and educators are likely to change and adapt quickly enough. Already the world—and the educators—are struggling to keep up.

210

For that reason, I believe much of this newly-named expanding/applying phase of growing-up will likely happen, for many, in a new venue—real and virtual—that arises alongside schools, as an alternative. My suggested name for these new places—both on Earth and in the Cloud—places where accomplishment and not learning is the goal—is **"Empowerment Hubs."** in the next chapter, I discuss what those are and can be.

The Curriculum Re-frame is to 2 Billion Individual Paths

But before we consider these Empowerment Hubs, I want to re-frame the notion of "curriculum." (Turn to Chapter 15 if you can't wait.)

There have been lists—unwritten and written—of things adults think young people should learn and know for a very long time. These are often called "curricula" and are unlikely to ever go away. For an amusing, fictional and satirical look at a prehistoric curriculum—and the difficulty of changing it—I highly recommend a quick perusal of the anonymous "Saber Tooth Curriculum" that can be found at https://bit.ly/3p7PGJC.

Early on in history curricula were likely informal, a combination of stories, lore, culture, and knowledge kept by shamans and others, and were different in scattered human cultures. The earliest curricula, as in the fictional story, probably included survival skills like hunting, fire-making, shelter-building, and migrating, as well as religious skills such as appeasing the gods.

Later curricula—often kept by parents and passed to their offspring—involved taming and raising animals and growing crops. Master craftsmen emerged, each having their own specific curricula for their apprentices, which were later codified by guilds. Informal curricula also existed regarding men's and women's' roles at each time, often passed among them informally and generationally.

Curricula became more formalized as early scholars founded Academies. From the ancient Greeks we got the trivium (grammar, logic, rhetoric) and the quadrivium (arithmetic, astronomy, music, geometry) which together form the "Seven Liberal Arts." The so-called Eastern world developed its own, such as the civil service curricula that grew out of Confucianism. Every religion in the world established its own curriculum to be taught to young members and converts. Places, and later nations, did the same.

Why?

Because our old world changed very slowly, and people needed to be replaced every generation, it became very important to pass down what we already knew about each role so it wouldn't have to be reinvented each time. The gradual increase in human knowledge along with the expansion of industrialism made it harder to do this only informally, or to only small groups—we required systematic ways to prepare "replacements" for every job or profession. Standard curricula were established —in the U.S. the standard high school curriculum was set by the so-called "Committee of 10" in 1894, and similar things happened in other places. Gradually we evolved the many specialized curricula (medicine, law, engineering, accounting, etc.) of today, often established and administered by the practitioners themselves, and often leading to standard, recognized credentials.

By the 20th century, the education curriculum in primary and secondary schools was fully established and codified—and it became very much the same the world over. It consisted, in the early years, of reading, and writing (of the local language) plus arithmetic, and then, in the "secondary" years, a combination of Math, Language, Science, History and Geography.

> **I call the standard secondary curriculum, in the English-speaking world,** *THE "MESS":* **M̲ath, E̲nglish, S̲cience, S̲ocial studies.**

There are local differences, emphases, and degrees of rigor, but with the exception of each being delivered in a local language, and the history tailored to each country (and its politics)—these differences are relatively minor. By the end of the 20th century, a "world curriculum" was in place almost everywhere. Although some did it for longer and more rigorously than others, *every 20th century school student went through it.*

Re-framing the World Curriculum

That, however, created a problem we now need to confront. Because many, after they spent years going through that curriculum, came to view it as "the universal truth" about what *all* young people should go through, be exposed to, and, ideally, learn and know to succeed in the world.

But the world had now changed. And unfortunately, this standardization—seen by many as a positive thing—**will not help our young people going forward**. The biggest re-framing of curriculum needed for the New Age of Empowerment is that

> **each individual person is best served by a separate, individual curriculum.**

For the New Age of Empowerment, the re-frame of our thinking about curriculum needs to be:

> *From standardized curricula for groups small or large,*
>
> **To each person having as their curriculum a unique, individual sequence of projects.**

This was something impossible in the past.

New Needs

Because we had limited resources and capabilities, we *had* to group people—and design curricula for them—by age, by subject, and level. Today there are a large number of curricula in the world, each developed in advance with some group and purpose in mind. Each student—or their parents—must choose one or several (or have them chosen for them) to go through from start to finish.

Yet however large the number of curricula we have may be, it is *trivial* in comparison of what we need. In the New Age of Empowerment, we need as many different curricula—21st century sequences of projects—as we have young people. Going forward, we need **2-3 billion curricula.** Not all written down with a scope and sequence determined in advance, as today, but rather curricula that grow organically for each individual, out of their current interests and prior achievements.

What is so exciting to me about the New Age of Empowerment we are entering into is that it is now totally possible to have such a unique "curriculum" for each individual young person.

But Aren't There Things *Everyone* Needs?

In the old frame, we certainly thought so—and the list was extensive. In addition to the "basics" and "The MESS," individual countries and cultures had their own ideas and norms, and put these into curricula both formal and informal, for all. Many places established standards, or ideals for every student to meet.

One such standard, in the 20th century, was text literacy. I once heard the Finnish Prime Minister explain that when they decided this literacy was useful for all, they, very practically, made it a requirement for marriage.

Re-framing Universal Knowledge

But what is necessary and universal for all now needs a serious re-frame in the New Age of Empowerment. I re-framed "new basics" in the previous chapter. As people going forward increasingly become Symbiotic Empowered Hybrids, more and more things formerly seen as fundamentally "human" will be delegated to our technology parts. This leaves room for other, previously-neglected skills and tasks—such as accomplishing in a new, hybrid way—to become necessary for all.

Today, too many educators and parents still focus—using their old frame—mainly on what they think is required for the "human part" of each individual, rather than on the symbiotic whole. Some see these universal human-side needs as interpersonal skills and so promote social-emotional learning. Some highlight particular human skills from the past as 21st century skills. Some promote technology skills, such as programming, separately.

But no matter which of these they choose—or even if they choose all—those 20th century-born people retain the old frame of putting things into young people in advance rather than letting the necessary skills and knowledge develop—as needed—through accomplishment.

I believe another useful way to re-frame curriculum is:

> *From a series of courses that put content and skills into young people in advance,*
>
> **To a system that successfully integrates knowledge, skills, and technology into young Symbiotic Empowered Hybrids through their continuous completion, as students, of world-improving projects.**

It is the *combination* of the New Symbiosis we discussed in Chapter 1, and the empowering beliefs we discussed in Chapter 4, that makes this new framing possible.

> **Making this particular re-frame is, I believe, one of the key universal and fundamental challenges of our times.**

New Ways of Doing Things

It is already clear that reading, writing, arithmetic, math, language, science, social studies—and in fact all of the academic disciplines considered important in the 20th century curriculum—will be done, to the extent they are needed in the mid-to-late 21st century, very differently from today. Learning *any* curricula in advance *in every one of these areas* is decreasing useful going forward. This evolution has already begun in many areas.

For example, reading and writing—even one's native language—are skills requiring years of formal curriculum. Yet most people can, without any formal training at all, speak and listen in their native language. That is something that comes to most humans naturally through interaction, and in the right environment, those skills can get very sophisticated quite early. Today, with the technology on one's personal smart phone, any text, in any language, can be read to you in your native language. Any any word or phrase you don't understand can be explained to you in a pleasant voice you choose. You can put into writing in any language, anything you want to say. You can perform any calculation you need—small or large—just by asking for it, and you can find, by asking verbally any fact, detail, and increasingly, argument and information at any complexity you need. Thus, with only your native automatic speaking ability, you can create, for yourself any curriculum you want. Now imagine all these capabilities extended by another 20 years of development. Given this, are using the years for learning reading and writing a good use of young people's time?

Here is another re-frame for the New Age of Empowerment:

From knowing what adults think you should (i.e., the school curriculum)

To knowing what to ask for in order to get something done that betters your world.

In the New Age of Empowerment, it is not *having* knowledge that counts, but increasingly *figuring out what knowledge you need* in order to accomplish something you want to. Few get this from a formal curriculum. Most get it from completing projects in the real world—i.e., from accomplishing with impact.

From Sequential Courses—To Sequential Projects

A curriculum, in academic schools, is a set of information and skills to be imparted, laid out in a, generally logical, scope and sequence. Academic courses are typically split into classes lessons, and activities. Academic teachers are trained to "cover" curricula by going through them in a linear, step-by-step fashion—not leaving anything out (unless they run out of time, which they almost always do). The underlying, old frame is what some call "just in case." Since you don't know exactly what you will be asked to do, it is better to have as much information as possible in your head as a result of its having been "covered" in front of you. The problem, of course, is that most of what is covered goes, after the test, NOT into your head, but—at very best—onto your bookshelf. Those who ever go back and re-read former textbooks are rare exceptions. But now every textbook—and all the world's bookshelves—are accessible by just asking a question of a personal device that all will soon have. Not just the books are accessible, but each individual sentence, idea, and fact, at any level of detail.

So the needed re-frame is

From learning large amounts in advance, "just in case,"

To learning as you need to in order to accomplish.

This includes even "background," or conceptual knowledge.

Re-framing Motivation for Empowerment

Humans, unless forced, generally have little interest in, and patience for, learning about things that are of interest to others but of no use or interest to them at the moment. In the old frame of fixed

218

curricula, therefore, some kind of "forcing"—or enticement—is almost always necessary. This is often referred to as motivation. Being forced *can* make some people do some things (this is known metaphorically as "the stick") And others are motivated by rewards (metaphorically "the carrot.") The carrot is often, these days, points and high scores in a so-called "gamified" system. But the only *empowering* motivation is wanting to accomplish something meaningful to you. This is sometimes known as "intrinsic" motivation. For the New Age of Empowerment, we can re-frame "motivation" like this

From getting people to care about things that they don't by finding external techniques that entice them,

To helping people continually find and accomplish things they <u>do</u> care about.

This is best done, I believe, by re-framing the entire concept of curriculum, i.e., of what gets offered to young people in what is now considered the school years in the following way:

From a series of sequential classes and courses,

To a series of sequential, accomplishments—of real, world-impacting projects.

Projects, chosen by the doers, that have a Measurable Positive Impact on some aspect of their world is what motivates most humans—very successfully—at all ages and in all contexts. Those projects (sadly today very few, if any) are what people typically remember from their school years, and are what has the most impact on their long-term success.

Don't "Projects" Need Preparation?

"But how can they do the projects," some ask, if they haven't taken the courses?" Or, put even more squarely in the old frame, "How can they do projects without knowing 'the basics'?" We already discussed how the basics are changing, but the answer to the question Do you have to know everything basic before you start accomplishing? is almost certainly no. In fact, it is often *not* knowing everything in advance that helps make projects, and accomplishing, valuable. How many meaningful projects did you ever do knowing everything about them in advance?

Sadly, the projects done in many schools within the old frame of courses—often called "Project-based Learning" (PBL)—are not very helpful. They are almost never done in the real-world outside of school, but are mostly different kinds of pedagogy and are actually "tests," designed to measure knowledge and conformance to standards. (We know this because people get paid large sums to identify the standards that various PBL projects check off.) Few PBL projects improve the real world in any meaningful way. Although called "projects" they are really just another pedagogy for stuffing-in the curriculum. Most of the school curriculum—whether it has been stuffed in through lectures, assigned reading, assigned PBL or other means—gets forgotten, generally right after any evaluation. But when a person improves the world—even in small ways—*they tend to remember it all their life.*

Empowerment Hubs

There is a new option for young people, an option just now emerging in the world, that allows this to happen, in a way that is helpful to both the individuals and the world they live in. That new option, and means is *doing continuous real-world projects* in what are known (at least initially) as Empowerment Hubs. In the next chapter we look at this emerging phenomenon, and how it will help young people prepare for the 21st century lives.

Harbingers

Amazingly, a true harbinger of the future of schools and curricula has been with us—locally praised but largely ignored—for more than 20 years. High Tech High (HTH) in San Diego CA (USA) was started in 2000 by Larry Rosenstock, with funding from the founders of Qualcomm as a true alternative to academic school. It has now grown to a family of 16 charter public schools, running from elementary to high school. From the beginning, High Tech High has been based on students doing almost entirely project-based work—as close to full-time as legally possible. HTH has made a real difference in its community—and has made efforts to spread its model through a different kind of teacher preparation. I believe their time has finally come.

Reflection Question

Do you think "the same schooling everywhere" and the current world curriculum are a good requirement for all young people? Would you support an alternative? If so, there now is one.

Chapter 17

INTRODUCING 'EMPOWERMENT HUBS'

From {Courses & Classes}
To [Real-World Projects with Impact]

YOUNG PEOPLE ARE FULL OF ENERGY. Their search for an alternative to sitting in class—a state that more and more young people find increasingly intolerable—has been going on for a long while. Other than working, being unemployed, or in some places joining a gang—all often worse—there have been almost no positive alternatives to school, and none fully supported by adults.

A Huge Waste of Resources

Once upon an agricultural time, most young people were actively accomplishing, helping mostly on family farms. But by the 20th century, life in most of the world didn't allow this. Young people, with all their energy and dreams, fell into a strange state where they couldn't contribute much productively (except by being exploited)—and often got in the way of their parents' work. The world badly needed a solution for the stage of life from roughly 6-21 years.

And the world came up with one—which was almost universally adopted. It was to lock the young people in schools and try to teach them what humans had previously discovered. Learning was the task adults decided young people must do—and we insisted they do— mostly, I believe, because it worked for so many of us in the 20th century. Adults could do this, despite any protests from the young people, because, in the frame we previously lived in adults were the young people's "owners." They just passed laws.

To be fair, adults thought that in doing this that they were helping both the young people and society. Even if many of the young people didn't like it, it was—like bad-tasking medicine— someday going to be "good for them." And that worked for a time, when the numbers going through school were smaller and less inclusive.

But as the numbers expanded school, as a solution, become less and less effective. More and more time needed to be spent on learning to view the past and keep up with the times. Even brief periods of "recess" were gradually reduced and even eliminated in some places. School became for many, essentially an incarceration. Really only two things got many young people through it—sports and friends—those are the only things young people have universally told me they like about school.

The result, for young people and for society has been an enormous waste of energy and resources—*those of almost half the world*—that could be far more usefully—and enjoyably— employed. They were not employed usefully, up until now, because we hadn't figured out how. But now we have.

The Move to Impactful Projects

As we enter the New Age of Empowerment, our fast-changing world is currently in the process of evolving from "continuously ongoing activities"—such as "school" or "jobs"—to shorter-term activities with closure and observable results, such as "projects." I see this as part of a general trend toward conciseness—a great many things are now more bite-sized, at all levels. Letters become Tweets. Books become Tik-toks. Companies are reframing "work"—as we will see in in Chapter 17—from "jobs" to "projects."

Many see this as a negative development, but I see it, rather, as part of a natural evolutionary process, responding to our faster-changing environment. Some schools have already started doing projects with their students, but as we just saw, this "PBL" is mostly just another form of pedagogy for the old learning process. it is not yet—with few exceptions—empowering. Nor does it put young peoples' energy to use in service of a better world. Yet now we have a way to do that.

For our young people to become empowered, and thrive in the New Age of Empowerment, we—and they—need to re-frame how young people spend their time in "preparation" for adulthood. I believe the needed re-frame in this area is this:

From needing to complete courses of study or job training as preparation for adulthood,

To continually completing real-world-impacting project after project—contributing, adding value, and successfully accomplishing—while picking up whatever they need for successful completion along the way.

To be meaningful and worthwhile in the New Age of Empowerment, all these projects need to relate to and involve each person's personal dreams, interests, uniqueness, talents, skills, and passions. This series of projects—i.e., sequential, successfully completed, self-chosen accomplishments—is what will matter in the New Age of Empowerment. In the expanding/applying stage of growing up it may be called their personal curriculum. During the rest of life, it will be known as work. In both cases it consists of real-world accomplishments with impact.

The projects, in both these cases, are both *unique* and *ad hoc*. They are created as required by, and for, each person and team. It is only when one finishes a project that one can really decide (with guidance) what the next one should be. Each person will have their own unique set of projects as they journey through the expanding/applying stage.

Starting these kinds of self-chosen, impactful projects early in life provides young people with not only the pleasure of doing them, and the teamwork skills necessary, but leads, very importantly, to the self-confidence that they *can* do them—each time with increasing sophistication. It also leads to clarity as to one's choice of projects, and of roles one wants to do as future work. It puts the vast energy of young people to use in ways that (a) they like, and (b) that benefit their world.

Where? Empowerment Hubs!

Where can such sequences of projects—in this re-framed "expanding" stage of growing up—best be done?

To some extent, some will be done in existing schools. There are a few schools, like the previously-mentioned High Tech High in San Diego, California (a charter public school) and a number of private

225

schools—such as the Riverside School in India and the Concept Schools in Brazil—that are already trying.

But schools, in most cases, remain firmly in the old frame of 20th century education, and are therefore generally difficult environments for doing the kinds of real, world-improving, student-selected projects young people need. Most of the projects schools offer do not inspire great outpourings of energy. As my 16-year-old son—once said to me "Only every once-in-a-lifetime does a project come around that you are actually interested in."

Although they have the captive kids, today's schools are not really good places for the kinds of projects we are talking about in this book. Perhaps that will change in the future. But such projects take varying amounts of time, and need flexible, variable schedules, while schools almost always have time constraints and strict schedules so that classes can be held. Schools often have physical limitations on what students can do—such as going out in the real world. In our current world, the projects we are talking about are, I believe, best done *outside* of school.

Several existing organizations, like Design for Change, 4H, and others, can, and already do, enable this. But it needs to become broader—and available to all. I strongly believe that to do the kinds of projects we are talking about in the New Age of Empowerment, a very different structure from our current academic "schools" is required. Having re-framed the period and process we now call "going to school" as "expanding/applying—i.e., "accomplishing"— both on Earth and in the Cloud, we now need a better, and fully-dedicated structure for doing these projects.

A New Alternative—Empowerment Hubs

We can now add a new, side-by-side alternative for young people and their parents during the expanding/applying phase of growing up, by re-framing what young people do in those years as follows:

From a sequence of academic courses and activities (i.e., from an academic education), done in schools (whether physical or online),

To a sequence of projects, done by worldwide teams—projects that are chosen by the teams and accomplished (with adult coaching) in Empowerment Hubs.

The Empowerment Hubs are not just a gradual evolution of academic schools, but a ***distinct, side-by-side alternative***. Just as with academic education, the work can happen in either the physical world (Earth) or in the Cloud, or a combination.

In this new Empowerment Hub alternative, these real-world projects become the primary occupation and time-occupier of young people during their Expanding phase of life.

No Need to *Abolish* Schools

This does NOT mean, importantly, abolishing schools for all. It is not at all my view that our current education should be abolished—nor, I believe, is it likely that it ever will be—because some will still want it and benefit from it. But that percentage is rapidly decreasing. Nor does it mean that a person who access to the knowledge previously stored in books can't still get it—they can and will always be able to.

Rather, I believe

> **there will exist—everywhere—an alternative set of places (a combination of real and virtual) for parents to send their children to for a far better preparation for the New Age of Empowerment.**

Today this does not exist in any unified way, but it is starting to exist in pockets. Empowerment Hubs are starting all over the world. It is time for them to emerge as a valid alternative for all the world's young people.

How are they Different?

This chart highlights some of the key differences between academic schools and Empowerment Hubs:

EMPOWERMENT HUBS: A SIDE-BY-SIDE ALTERNATIVE FOR DIGITAL NATIVES	
ACADEMIC SCHOOLS...	EMPOWERMENT HUBS...
- 20c. vision of what we needed	- 21st c. vision of what we now need
- Focus on "academic learning"	- Focus on Accomplishment w/Impact
- 80+% classes, some "learning projects"	- 80+% Real-World Projects
- Measure "learning progress"	- Measure Impact
- Focus on Individual work	- Focus on Teams, Networking & Collab.
- Technology an optional "tool"	- Technology a Symbiotic Part
- "Mastery certification" for later	- Cont's (real-world) Accomplishment NOW
- Maybe "Potential" Empowerment	- Actual (Applied) Empowerment

A Precedent

There has already been one (20th century) precedent, and success for the kind of change we are trying to make—it is Montessori schools. In the early 1900s, Maria Montessori, a physician, had a different vision for what primary age school kids should be doing, and established places to do it ("Montessori Schools") which grew into a worldwide alternative movement. Today—in many places, if they can afford it—a parent with a primary school aged child will almost certainly ask themselves: "Is my child a good fit for academic school or for Montessori?"

That is precisely the question we hope young people and their parents will all be able, and required, to ask themselves in the future:

"Am I (if a young person), or is my child, a good fit for, and better off in, an academic school of some kind— or in an Empowerment Hub?"

Hopefully, in the time between now and 20 years in the future these will be formed, grow, and provide that alternative. The world's initial Empowerment Hubs now exist on every continent. Once they are established everywhere, then the marketplace—i.e., parents and young people—will be able to choose. I strongly believe the choice for most will be toward the Hubs and Empowerment, because they fit the needs of the young people in the New Age of Empowerment so much better.

And today, because we no longer have to build physical buildings but can create many of our initial Empowerment Hubs in the Cloud—we don't have to wait.

Creating Empowerment Hubs

Who will create these Empowerment hubs? Here is an important re-frame in this regard:

> *From education places created only by, and run only by, officially recognized educational experts (e.g., ministries, teachers),*
>
> **To the job of empowering young people moving to everyone.**

The old, 20th century frame of "academic education" requires a large, professional class of educators—teachers, administrators, teacher trainers. They all have to be trained and certified by governments and accreditation boards. Getting permission to run a school yourself, or even to teach in one, is often a difficult and complex task, as can be seen by all the barriers that are placed on creating "charter schools" in the U.S.

But it needn't be that way.

> _Everyone_ *can, and should, contribute to young peoples' preparation for their 21st century lives through coaching in, or starting and running, Empowerment Hubs.*

This is not a pie-in-the-sky idea. We already do it—and know much about how to do it well—from many successful programs from Scouts, to 4H, to First Robotics. What we need are more ways to help those getting started, and a common, "umbrella," non-trademarked name for the movement under which all

"Empowerment Hubs," of all kinds, can flourish. That is now arriving.

What Happens in these Empowerment Hubs?

It is, in principle, very simple.

> **Participants do continuous real-world projects of their own choosing, in small teams coached by adults using one of many existing and successful processes, to get to, for each project, a Measurable Positive Impact on some aspect of the world outside the team.**

The results are collected as a resume of accomplishments for each participant. There are an infinite number of ways to do this, and each Empowerment Hub, or group of Hubs, will find its own.

In every case, the goal for participants is only to:

> **Accomplish in the world with the Measurable Positive Impact that you chose.**

The Global Ministry of Empowerment, Accomplishment, and Impact

Who will curate and guide this process? Every country in the world, today, has a Ministry (or Department) of Education to do this. Many smaller places within countries, such as states, districts, or cities, often have their own. *But there are, currently, no Ministries of Empowerment.*

There needs to be, and I predict there soon will be. Why separate ministries from education? Empowering young people is not really the province of an education department, because getting an academic education is a very different thing than expanding/applying via empowerment, accomplishment and having positive impact on the world. The new alternative requires its own places for encouragement and oversight.

> **That is why I have started—with colleagues from every continent—the Global Ministry of Empowerment, Accomplishment, and Impact (<u>ministry-of-eai.org</u>). Our not-for-profit aim is to promote, facilitate and support the creation of Empowerment Hubs everywhere.**

We are a growing group of people—young and old—excited about the New Age of Empowerment and the new re-frame for raising young people. Our intention is to be more of an unleashing mechanism than a standards body. All that is required to join us is a commitment to empowering young people—of any age—though their doing continuous real-work projects with real impact on their world.

The motivation for creating this Global Ministry was our common discovery that—as we presented the Empowerment Hub concept and frame to people inside and outside of education— more and more everywhere wanted to participate. We hope to be their initial guide to help them get started and flourish. Our vision is that the new Empowerment frame for raising young people will spread quickly both around the Cloud, and to countries, places, and individuals all over the globe—much as Montessori's new frame did. Is our intention to give all of these empowerment hubs as much guidance as they need to succeed.

What is the Relevant Time Frame?

Empowerment Hubs have already started to appear in the Cloud and on all continents (for current information on these, see the ever-growing website: ministry-of-eai.org). How long will take for Empowerment Hubs (or whatever they are eventually known as) to become a viable alternative to academic schools around the world? It is, of course, impossible to say, but things are moving quickly—it could take as little as a decade. The biggest barrier is the old frame that so many adults carry with them. It is to help break that old frame that I have written this book.

Individual Startups

The best way to start an empowerment hub, if you want to, is to just do it. Depending on where you live, your Hub may or may not be able to be certified as a full-time alternative to school. But it can certainly be started after-school and on weekends. We have created online an ever-updating "how-to" manual for those who want to do this. You can find it at http://bit.ly/empowerment-today .

Inside Companies?

Another interesting place for Empowerment Hubs to be set up is inside existing companies—for both employees' children, neighborhood children, and even for employees. This would afford great opportunities for both employees and young people to work on projects in multi-generational—and in many cases worldwide—teams.

Harbingers

The very first group that designated itself an Empowerment Hub—right after the term was invented by the 20-year-old Leo Wölfel in 2020, was Planet Pilots (http://planetpilots.org. Planet Pilots grew out of the Exponential Organizations (ExO) movement started by Salim Ismael. Planet Pilots founders are from Denmark, Colombia, Poland, and Vietnam, and it serves young people, online, from all over the world. A second Empowerment Hub has been established by the Riverside School in Ahmadabad, India. (https://schoolriverside.com/). A third is the Santa Maria School in Columbia (working with Planet Pilots.) Yet another upcoming Empowerment Hub is being started by SEK international schools, based in Spain. (https://www.sek.es/en/sek/about-us/).

The newly founded Ministry of Empowerment, Accomplishment and Impact is, we hope. a harbinger of similar ministries being set up by governments in every country.

And of course. Maria Montessori was a true harbinger in setting up in the 20th century, the first widespread alternative to academic education.

Reflection Question

Would you like to start, be part of, or contribute to an Empowerment Hub? What kind of Empowerment Hub would you like to be part of? Contact ministry-of-eai.org if interested.

Chapter 18

RE-FRAMING ASSESSMENT FOR THE NEW AGE OF EMPOWERMENT

From {Grades and Ranking}
to [Before & After + Measurable Positive Impact]

A GREAT MANY PEOPLE WORRY ABOUT ASSESSMENT. "You have to have a position on assessment" my mentor once told me.

There are many positive reasons for assessing performance—our own, or another's. But we do have to be careful not to do harm in the process. If, in the future, each person has a completely unique skill set, and each follows a completely unique curriculum of projects—*and* we don't want to do harm in the process—how will we assess people? Can we re-frame assessment in a less harmful and more empowering way?

The Old Frame

In the old frame, which is still in use today, "being assessed," is generally something to be feared. Very few like taking a test or getting a performance review. I can still remember my own fear when, as a new teacher, my supervisor showed up at the back of my classroom, or when I thought I would fail the exams and flunk out of Harvard Business School, even though almost no one does, and I wound up getting honors.

One reason for this fear is that, in the old frame, assessment is almost entirely competitive. Some make it and some don't. If the assessment is done by ranking, either explicitly or implied, there is only a single number one or, at best, a narrow cut-off. When there are only a few winners, everyone else is a loser.

One reason this competitive situation occurs is because everyone is generally being assessed on the same thing—we don't assess *what* you did, but rather *how* you did. And we often make it quantitative: We have "summative" assessments (often just a number), "formative" assessments (where we tell you why your number wasn't high enough, and how to increase it next time) and "ipsative" assessments (where we ask whether you beat your own number from last time.) In addition, assessment too often focuses on your so-called "weaknesses," rather than on your strengths.

No wonder most are afraid of being assessed.

Does Data Help?

Some think numerical data and quantitative assessment make the process better, or fairer. While qualitative assessment was once the norm, we live, today, in a very data-driven frame, that values computer-analyzable data in particular. Many have come to focus almost entirely on quantitative measures when assessing because numeric data—relevant or not—is now so much easier to collect, store and analyze.

Some see this as empowering. But I think it is precisely the opposite—most assessment is *dis*empowering. The people who believe it *is* empowering often use the phrase "If you can't measure it, you can't manage it." But that phrase is not completely true —in either direction. There are many things we can't measure accurately—love, empathy, hate, and more—and yet we can find ways to increase or decrease them. And, far too often, what we do carefully measure are only "proxies," i.e., substitutes that we *can* more easily manage (e.g., grades, graduation rates) standing in place of the important things we can't measure easily or directly (e.g., learning or success.)

The result is that we end up with quantitative assessments based on numbers that don't really matter. Qualitative assessments are often far more comprehensive and nuanced—but they, in turn, are frequently dismissed as being potentially biased.

Keep the Nuance, Eliminate the Bias

What we want, of course, is to keep the nuance, while minimizing the bias. There was supposedly a sign hanging on Albert Einstein's office wall reading: "Not everything can be counted, and not everything that can be counted counts." It is unhelpful to dismiss all, or most, qualitative assessments in favor of only the quantitative. Although the quantitative may be quicker, more numerically precise, and with technology much easier to do—it does not always produce the useful, or unbiased, results we want. Today in education we collect data on a great many things: attendance, test scores, grades, graduation rates and more. These are easy to count, but their value in assessing people's future performance is, at very best, suspect. We perform all sorts of analyses of this data, but we still often don't know whether a person —after decades of school—can accomplish anything useful in the real world. This is a big reason that why hiring remains such a difficult issue.

"Ranking Kills"

A far too often-used form of assessment is "ranking." Ranking makes it easier to fill a limited number of slots with, supposedly, the "best" people—they are assumed to be those at or near the top. But true, accurate ranking of people is really impossible—except in simple cases, such as multiple-choice exams which lack nuance. In real-life performance there are so many factors that no one can accurately determine exact rankings of individuals, particularly over broad categories. Yet many still try—there are whole industries devoted to ranking—truly, I believe, wasting time and money. And there are still plenty of "competitions" with winners (and mostly losers). In extreme cases, rankings can, literally, lead to death. Poorer-than-desired school rankings have led to young people throwing themselves out of windows (in Korea), or throwing themselves under trains (in Palo Alto, California).

We can and should, I believe, re-frame ranking:

From a useful way to assess,

To something almost impossible to do accurately—and more harmful than not.

For most purposes, ranking is not even necessary—having only three categories, or "buckets," is enough: (1) Adequate or satisfactory performance (the vast majority, maybe 80 percent), (2) Extraordinary performance (maybe 10 percent), and (3) Not yet ready (maybe 10 percent.) Those are the assessment categories used at the Harvard Business School, for example. They allow for a useful separation of people—particularly when summed along multiple dimensions—without introducing unneeded competition.

Bettering the World

Fortunately, in the New Age of Empowerment, there is at least one much better way to assess useful competence. A far better frame for and method of assessment is one of *improvement or bettering—* not—as in "ipsative" assessment— just of yourself, *but of the world around you.*

With the coming in the New Age of Empowerment of "completed world-improving projects" as the unit of achievement, rather than "grades in courses"—assessment of what a person can do actually *becomes easier*—because we can watch them do it.

The necessary re-frame for this new kind of assessment is

From Scores, Grades, and Rankings,

To Measurable Positive Impact on some aspect of the world.

"Before and After"

What we are trying to produce, remember, is Good, Empowered, World-Improving people. An assessment re-frame that will help us more consistently produce them is:

From comparatively ranking people based on complex tests and other current procedures,

To simply looking at "Before and After."

What we want is for all people, of any age, to be able to point to something—small or large—and say:

> *"See that? Last year it was bad (or didn't exist.) Now it's much better. I and my team did that."*

All We Need to Know

It really is very simple. All we really want—and need—to know in the New Age of Empowerment is "Did some aspect of the world improve because of you (and your team)?" —NOT "Did you do it better than someone else?"

Because everyone is being assessed as a unique individual (and every team as unique), what improves, and how it improves will be different in each case. The improvements—i.e., accomplishments—can then get listed on a "resume of accomplishments" that every person builds while growing up—and continues building for the rest of their life. We can all—as employers or in other roles—then look at those and make our judgments—*not* about the relative worth of the people—or even the relative worth of particular impacts and improvements they made—but on *the kinds of improvements we are looking for, and those people's unique ability to make them.*

Measurable Positive Impact

The metric I therefore suggest we use for projects is ***Measurable Positive Impact*** (MPI).

"Measurable," in this case, does not mean you can necessarily assess it quantitatively—it means something *actually happened*—some improvement took place that is observable by others. This is not as hard as one might think—most people know improvement when they see it, and if they disagree on the margins, they can use consensus.

> *In the new frame, no project is completed—or assessed as complete—unless it can demonstrate a Measurable Positive Impact (MPI).*

It is the unique combination, and total, of the improvements each person makes—on whatever scale and in whatever way they can—that defines someone as a good, empowered, symbiotic, world-improving human of the future.

Harbingers

An example of future forms of assessment is *Design for Change*, an organization now in over 60 countries. (http://dfcworld.org). They share the success of their young participants' (ages 3-20) team projects by making videos—typically made by the project team—that show what they accomplished, the process they went through, and the result. The videos show how they did each stage of the process (which they call "Feel-Imagine-Do-Share") as well as the projects' Measurable Positive Impact. Design for Change now has tens of thousands of these videos and projects, and while some are highlighted, they are in no way "ranked." When in 2019, Design for Change gathered 3000 young people at a conference in Rome (with the Pope), it was not to give prizes, but rather for the teams to share their projects with each other—which they did on school stages throughout the Eternal City.

Reflection Question

Have YOU seen any young people's projects with Measurable Positive Impact on the world? (Please send word about any you know of to marcprensky@gmail.com). Can you think of such projects that might be useful and fun for some young people to do?

Chapter 19

RE-FRAMING 'HIGHER EDUCATION' FOR THE NEW AGE OF EMPOWERMENT

From {Getting credentialled}
To [Finding Peers]

IN THE 20ᵀᴴ CENTURY A GREAT MANY THOUGHT that getting more than a secondary education and obtaining a tertiary educational degree at a college or university was always better for a young person—and a great many still do. They often cite statistics showing that on average one will earn considerably more over one's lifetime if one has at least a bachelor's degree—and even more with a masters or doctorate. In citing those true figures from the 20th century, they are, unfortunately, projecting those statistics into the 21st century as predictors. That may be a big mistake.

Given our new re-frames of learning (in Chapter 9) and of the school years (in Chapter 13) it is important that we now also re-frame what is called higher (or tertiary) education for the New Age of Empowerment, using the same twenty-year timeframe. What will higher education for young people, roughly 18-22, look like in 2040? Many academics are wondering anxiously about this, holding symposia and panels all over the world to discuss it. I have been part of several of these. As you should, by now, expect, I add a different perspective and re-frame.

What is the Need?

Currently, we spend huge sums of money (either from parents' paying private tuition or from government subsidies) for young people to attend these places. We do this because we think—or thought—that more education is always better—*and* because the credential of a higher education degree is still used as a resume-culling strategy by many employers. The question now on everybody's mind is "Is it worth the time and cost"? Or does higher education require a big re-frame as well? I believe it does.

I would re-frame higher (or tertiary) education

From a place where people trade money and time for future earning power,

To a sorting mechanism for finding useful peers.

I believe that in practice higher education is already the latter—although few talk about it that way. Education today, through secondary school and roughly age 18 is mostly done locally with those who happen to live near you. Then, right around age 18, young people are sorted—or self-sorted—into "peer groups" through the college and university admissions process (or though the job search.)

'The Great Sort'

Through the 20th century young people rarely expanded beyond their local town, or city borders. Then, in many of the societies of the late 20th century, a "great human sort" began to happen when those young people—who had been constrained up until then to interacting almost entirely with the young people and families in the area where they grew up—got distributed (sorted)— into a new mix, in colleges and universities for higher education around countries and the world (and thence possibly into professions.) Many, at this point got sorted out of the academic system and immediately into jobs.

Some of this kind of sorting had always been happening for the wealthy—their young people were often distributed between various elite schools at home or abroad. In the 20th century university attendance—and the sorting it brought—became much more widespread. As the number going to higher education swelled—particularly after WWII in the U.S—it was increasingly necessary to sort people into the "proper" places.

That "proper place" turns out to be "with your peers"—however you define them. The people who did the most defining of these categories—usually out of the spotlight—were the college and university admissions officers and committees. Their goal was to create each year a class of people who "belonged" at that school. Some sorted by the students' class in society. Some sorted by intellectual prowess or test scores. Some sorted by sports or even partying. But getting in to a place counted far more than getting out. Getting out counted, of course, for having a degree or credential— but getting in counted for the "value" of that degree in the marketplace and in society.

Many young people, of course, did not participate in the sort at all, skipping higher education for immediate jobs (another kind of sort). But as the world began to see higher education as something necessary for young people's success, more and more wanted and entered the academic sorting process.

Many assumed that the reason we did this sort, in every country, was for each young person's individual *intellectual* development, i.e., to put them into the place most appropriate for their learning progress and development. But let me suggest a re-frame which, as I said, is already taking place:

From college and university as something needed for individuals' intellectual development,

To college and university as a sorting of the population into "peer groups" and a way for people to spend formative years with that group of peers.

In Loco Parentis

A view of higher education institutions half a century ago when I was there, was that they served *in loco parentis* (i.e., in the place of parents) during the time the young people attended, i.e., as parental caretakers. While that doctrine may be less used today, what is interesting is that, in that sense, ***the institutions are parents who choose you.*** By applying, you let them know that you want them to be the parents that you couldn't choose earlier and by accepting you, they agree to this.

Once we have this new frame—and see Higher Education as a sorting mechanism, rather than as a provider of anything really needed by young people beyond the name of the institution and its diploma—entirely new options arise for society. If sorting is a useful goal, we can begin to search for new sorting mechanisms that are better suited for, and make more sense in, the New Age of Empowerment.

We Do the Sort Because Peer Groups are Empowering

The current sort doesn't always work, as well as it should, for every person. It certainly involves many rejections. But when the sort works well, it can be quite empowering. You are empowered far more by which peer group (college or university) you are sorted into than by whatever professors you happen to get. Many schools sort students even more finely, for further empowerment, into fraternities, sororities, and secret societies. It was certainly empowering for me to be sorted into Harvard and Yale for graduate school.

It is already clear that in the New Age of Empowerment there are new ways both to sort and be sorted. More of it can be done, with enterprise, by yourself. Some use the term "finding your tribe" for this sorting process. I'm not personally a fan of the term tribe— tribes tend to fight with each other— but it is another way of saying "the group in which you feel comfortable, and feel you belong"— i.e., your peer group. Finding this group, and spending a number of years with them, away from home, at a particularly formative time of life—i.e., adolescence—can be enormously empowering for your entire professional life.

Now Worldwide, in the Cloud

In the New Age of Empowerment there are entirely new possibilities for doing the sort, on a worldwide basis, both in the Cloud and in person. One new university—Minerva— already puts together a cohort of talented people from around the world that every 3-4 months relocates (when not constrained by Covid) to a different continent. A young person can certainly find peers, already, in on-line programs. In 20 years, I predict there will be far more ways to find peer groups. Like online dating, this is just in its infancy. By then peers will be able to sort on multiple dimensions and get together from all over the world. I predict the world will no longer need universities and other tertiary institutions to perform this task.

What it Means

What that means, for the institutions, is that they will have to make their purpose far more specific. Today, per Michael Crow, president of ASU, which aspires to be a model for the future) higher learning institutions do three things:

1. Universities—particularly the top ones—provide basic, non-applied, research. We need this, as the research governments and industry do is often directed to their specific needs. How this will be funded is an open question.

2. Residential Colleges and Universities provide a multi-year experience with peers. A great many young people in the world look forward to this. It coincides with the formative period of their later adolescence and provides a relatively safe place to explore one's independence without great responsibility.

3. A variety of tertiary institutions provide knowledge and skills, online and off. This function is becoming more and more specific, as people seek job-specific skills—and as the "well rounded person" ceases to be the ideal (or even possible). It is now breaking down into individual "competencies", and we see companies like Google, Microsoft and Cisco taking over part of this function with certifications. [26]

A Higher Education Re-Frame

Higher education is struggling financially—the current tuition system—at least in the U.S.—is almost certainly untenable. My hope and sense is that we will find new ways to fund late adolescents' getting together productively.

One option is that, as we move to Empowerment Hubs and projects, tertiary institutions will continue this kind of empowerment into the tertiary years. Imagine what young people, already empowered by 12 years of accomplishing real, world-impacting projects could do if the doing of such projects were extended, with all the project experience the young people and their coaches will have, into the years between 18 and 25.

But it may turn out that 12 years of projects—and discovering their unique value-add—may be enough for most young people to enter the work force. At which point with peer-groups findable elsewhere, a residential college experience will be only for those who seriously want to do research, or for those whose families can afford for them to spend the time partying.

Harbingers

I have always seen Northeastern University, headquartered in Boston (USA) — founded on the unique idea of "engagement with the world," rather than on being an "ivory tower" —as a harbinger for the future of higher education. All students are required to work on real-world projects in their "signature": co-op program. A very positive sign is that Northeastern has recently been expanding into other cities around the US and the globe, including London, Charlotte, Portland, San Francisco, Seattle, Silicon Valley, Vancouver, and Toronto. Hopefully, their model's time has come.

Reflection Question

Is getting *into* college (i.e., being sorted with your peers) more important than getting out?

Chapter 20

RE-FRAMING WORK FOR THE NEW AGE OF EMPOWERMENT

From {Doing Jobs}
to [Adding Unique Value to Projects]

THE END OF GROWING-UP IS, IDEALLY, FULL-TIME WORK. If you get there, the good part is having your own income—and what that allows for you and for your family. Not getting there is often very painful. But even if you do get to full-time work, it is for many people—possibly most—not a particularly happy experience. In fact, as much as they might want the income, young people would probably agree that most work "sucks"—as do most jobs.

Can we re-frame and change this in the New Age of Empowerment? Hopefully.

Today, Work = Stress

The stress level of today's working world extremely is high in many places. First there is the stress of figuring out what you want to *do* as work. That part will become even more stressful going forward by the fact that "replacement" is going away in many places and areas. Then there is the stress of actually finding a job you want—we do not make that task easy. It was hard for me even graduating from Harvard Business School—I was so stressed outby my job search that I forgot a wedding I was supposed to attend! The stress will only go up as automation and A.I. change employer's needs, and as our population continues in uneven ways, to increase. Once you get a job—almost any job—there is "starting at the bottom." No matter where you went to school you are unlikely to have learned how to accomplish much in the real world. When you finally get employed, you have to begin a second education all over again (this is sometimes called training or professional development.) Much of it happens on-the-job. And every time you rise a level (if you do) there is the additional stress of learning a new role.

But apart from all that stress, there is for most, the stress of *doing something you really don't want to be doing.* Many people— possibly most— do not love—and even actively hate—their jobs. Those that do truly love what they do for a living are a small, lucky, exception—most would say that their actual, daily job "sucks," probably using that very vernacular. The country song "You Can Take This Job and Shove It" reached number 1 on the charts.

I have often thought that the compensation you get in return for a job is not for the work, but *for the stress*—and is often—although not always—proportional to its degree.

Different?

For coming generations, in the New Age of Empowerment, that will hopefully be different. The reason is a re-framing of what work is. In the New Age of empowerment "work" is being re-framed as not just a "job", but as meaningful *activity to you*. We can re-frame the work phase of life

> *From doing a job mainly to get a paycheck,*
>
> **To doing something that realizes some part of your dreams.**

Not all of everyone's dreams will, of course, ever be fully realized. But in the New Age of Empowerment many more will than in the past. We saw in the "FAR Better" model of growing up empowered, (on page 150) that realizing dreams is both the motivation for, and the result of, spending the expanding years applying one's uniqueness (i.e., one's unique dreams, interests, skills, passions, and value-add) to world-improving projects. We can, in New Age of Empowerment re-frame the "working" stage as the period of **Realization** of many of—and hopefully our biggest—dreams.

Realizing Dreams

The "realizing" (i.e., adult) stage is where most people spend the bulk of their life—all young people, barring tragedy, grow up to get there. Already, in the early 21st century, that stage is much longer than it was in the past; with new advances in science, today's young people's adult stage will likely be even longer.

But up until now being an adult was not, for most, a time of dream realization—in many places the only realizable dream was having a large family. "Big" dreams got realized only for a lucky few—those who became stars or rose to the top of a hierarchy or profession. Some did achieve a dream of becoming wealthy, or rich. But we all know of unhappy rich or famous people.

What IS Success?

I think a goal for every young person has always been to become a "successful" adult, but success will likely never have a universal definition. The meaning of "successful" needs re-framing for each era—and possibly for each person. At one point, and in some places, success could be achieved by having a home, a family, and a job, and being part of a local community. Some have always defined success in terms of personal wealth, or achievement.

Success in the New Age of Empowerment

What will "being successful" mean in the mid-to-late 21st century? It will likely be a time replete with automation and artificial intelligence, plus symbiotic empowered people. Is there a useful way to re-frame "adult success" for our New Age of Empowerment?

My definition of human success has always included becoming a "good," "empowered," and "world-improving" person, and so I'll start there. My re-frame for successful adulthood in the New Age of Empowerment is:

From having a home, a family, and a job in a local community,

To a being a good, empowered, and world-improving person in the world.

I believe each of the parts—good, empowered, and world-improving—needs its own re-framing for the New Age of Empowerment.

Good

I will not attempt to define "good" here—you can decide on your own definition. But I would suggest re-framing the good part of being successful in the New Age of Empowerment as moving from being locally good to globally good, i.e.,

> *From conforming to your local community and cultural standards, whatever they may be,*
>
> **To having Love, Gratitude, and Empathy for all, everywhere, and doing the most good and least harm one can in the world.**

My sense is that humans, and the world, are becoming more and more unified in defining what is "good" —with some obvious exceptions. A term for success that many are using these days is "well-being"—which some equate with "happiness." Countries such as Bhutan are already trying to measure and increase this.

Empowerment, World-Improvement and Meaningful Work

The "empowered" and "world-improving" parts of success, however, are most often defined through what we call work.

Most humans, I assert, are not content being idle most of the time—they prefer having something meaningful to do—i.e., meaningful to them. Success comes when they are able to get something meaningful done—whatever it may be—and from seeing that it impacts, and improves, their world, and people they care about, in some positive way. A good indicator of growing up successfully—although not the only one—is that you are able to earn a living throughout your lifetime—at least most of the time—through work that is meaningful to you and that you love to do

Sadly, not everyone in the world has this today. But I think there is greater hope for the future.

Re-framing Work as Adding Value

Today, with the growing inequality in the world, and the coming of A.I. and automation, many around the globe are pessimistic about the future of work— as it is often called. That future—and that work—in most of these discussions, is most often framed in terms of employers, and their future needs, i.e., jobs. Will they exist? Will there be enough of them? What will they be?

But that might not be the right way to frame "work" for the future. What if we tried reframing it around today's young peoples' future needs?

"Having a job" is the old frame for work. Typically, in the 20th century, that meant a permanent, salaried or hourly job that a young person had to first prepare for, then find, and then keep doing for the rest of their working life. In the early 21st century, that frame become *many* jobs, *many* preparations, and in many cases continuous, sometimes fruitless, searching. That often-difficult frame will certainly continue, in part, into the mid-to-late 21st century, with many—still in that old frame—being employed in newly emerged jobs, with new titles and content, many of which are yet to be invented.

But, as new forms of work appear, the usefulness of the entire old "jobs" frame in the New Age of Empowerment is now open to reassessment. What we need to re-assess and re-frame is what "work" actually means.

Adding Unique Value

Here is my re-frame of work for the New Age of Empowerment:

> *From work being about "jobs."*
>
> **To work, going forward, being about ADDING UNIQUE VALUE, mostly in teams, and completing useful projects.**

Continuing to frame work as jobs scares many 20th-century-born people, because we are in such a transition regarding what jobs are and will be. Many young people ask: "Will there *be* jobs when I grow up? What will they entail? "Will I be able to do what is required?"

Yet I believe much of the current "future of work" discussion frightens people unnecessarily—both adults, and young people alike.

A Time for Uniqueness and Matching

Our notion of jobs comes out of the industrial era, when jobs, and roles were *fungible*—anyone with the right training could do them. But because each human is completely unique in their concerns, passions and strengths and capabilities, each has a *unique way* they can add value to teams, companies, and the world. I call this their "unique value-add." We are now able to not only understand this unique value add better, but finally begin to take full

255

advantage of it. As we now approach a point, in the New Age of Empowerment, where young people start to understand, far earlier in their lives, the ways they are unique, and the unique ways they can add value to projects (as well as the kinds of situations where they enjoy adding that value) we will start to see emerge, I believe, a new definition of work as "value-adding," and a new process for matching needs and value-adders.

A New Definition

I believe "work" in the New Age of Empowerment, work will be now seen as

> **an activity into which you put effort, add value, and get something in exchange of value to you.**

Some people's unique value-adding may be done in structured roles and in workplaces that are ongoing and longer term (i.e., "jobs")—but much of it won't. Some of it will be compensated directly and some indirectly (e.g., through Universal Basic Income and other social plans.) Today we are watching the world of work reshape itself.

Jobs are an Artifact

Although some always will find jobs, and be able to do what is required for them, my sense is that for many of today's young people the "what job will you have?" question doesn't even matter. Their future is not seen by them—as was ours throughout the 20th century—about fulfilling employers' requirements. Today's young people are entering into a world where what matters most is applying their uniqueness and invention, not preparation or replacement. The new world is about adding value in your own unique way. 21st century people can best help the world—and their employers—by finding and being themselves in terms of their unique value-add.

Humanity, as I said at the start of this book, will *never* run out of dreams to realize, problems to fix, people who need help or people who want to help them. In the New Age of Empowerment, doing that—realizing dreams, fixing problems, helping people—is what the future of work is.

How will this happen?

Up through the 20th century, we often differentiated between jobs—where what you get in exchange is money (sometimes with satisfaction and sometimes not)—and hobbies, artistic endeavors, and volunteering—where what you get in exchange, more often, is non-monetary satisfaction. Those two are now blending. In the emerging new "gig economy" many will get to do what were formerly art, hobbies, and volunteering as their work. Individual crafters, for example, can easily sell their work on etsy and eBay. Patreon enables individuals to find support for creative ventures. It is easy to publish or set up a business on your own. One of the first lucrative new gigs to emerge is people showing each other, online, in podcasts and coaching sessions, how do what they have successfully done in these areas. For larger projects, involving many skills, movie production has long had an effective model, where a crew of specialists is assembled for the length of each project and then disbanded. This is often far easier to do In the Cloud and can include people from many more places.

I propose two particular re-frames that we should communicate to young people regarding work:

> *From finding "a job" or jobs,*
>
> **To identifying and doing or joining projects where you add unique value.**

That is the new work goal for young people in the 21st century.

The corollary is a re-frame:

> *From doing whatever brings you the most money,*
>
> **To doing only work you find meaningful, and that you are enthusiastic about.**

I believe both of these will become possible for most in the New Age of Empowerment, i.e., within the next 20 years. Many young people are already realizing that even when you need money, you no longer have to do—and it is no longer worth doing—work you hate or dislike just to get it. Once you have identified your uniqueness and unique value-add, more and more ways will exist for you to find work you do like and find meaningful.

Harbingers

Several harbingers have appeared regarding the future of work in the form of new models. One model is gig work replacing full-time jobs. Another is round-the world work (originally done in software companies), where projects move continuously from time zone to time zone. We are seeing startups like Fivr provide the beginnings of better worldwide matching of unique value-adders and needs. Technology and the Cloud are the big enablers of these; their promise is just starting to be realized.

Today much effort is being expended in finding new ways (using A.I for example) to quickly train people to fill the holes employers have. Etsy, on the other hand, which is one of the fastest-growing platforms, is an example of starting with the value people are already adding.

Reflection Question

Where do *you* add value? Is that value unique to you? How can you help others add or create value? Are there new opportunities for your children (and you) in the New Age of Empowerment?

PART V

RE-FRAMING HUMANITY IN THE NEW AGE OF EMPOWERMENT

From {Individuals made In God's Image}
To [a Collective Mind and Species]

Chapter 21

TOWARD A COLLECTIVE MIND & SPECIES

I WANT TO END THIS BOOK by asking a bigger re-framing question:

> *"What is the best way to frame 'humanity' for maximum usefulness in the New Age of Empowerment?"*

Does humanity itself need a more useful re-frame?

My answer is it does. And my sense, and hope, is that the people who happen to be young today will do it.

Is "Being Human" Positive or Negative?

Being human, as Hamlet soliloquizes and as James Paul Gee describes in more detail in his book *What is a Human?*,[27] has, in addition to whatever is positive, many negatives. But up until now, being human was not something any person could seriously change, or "opt-out" of, other than by ceasing to exist. Up until now we were all bound, while here, by something often called our "human nature."

Humans have dealt with this, in the past through "shared myths" —Yuval Noah Harari's term [28] that put humans firmly at the top of the global hierarchy—exceeded only by "gods" we perceived or created. People are very proud of being human—we love to build monuments to ourselves glorifying our past, museums to document our past achievements, and to give each other prizes—of which there are many, from Nobel on down.

The key frame for humanity, up through the 19th century, was, I submit, "God's Image." You could take your pick among several alternative variations of this god, but each represented an ideal that individual humans could strive toward.

"Humanism"

In the 20th century, although God's Image persisted, the main frame of humanity shifted, and became "humanism." Humanism is the belief that humans, alone, are the best and most important thing in the universe (at least in terms of what we have discovered), and that everything should therefore be done—above all else—to benefit people. Harari calls humanism the current world's "overarching religion and belief." It leads to movements like "sustainability" which are selfishly human-centric. (Why should humans give up a good thing?)

Those two frames, In God's image and humanism— are still the ones most people use for humanity today.

Two Possible Re-frames

But here are two possible re-frames for humanity:

> *From a world where humans or God are on top,*
>
> **- To a big destructive "amoeba" in the universe**
>
> *OR*
>
> **-To a world where things—including humanity—can be re-designed to benefit all.**

How Good *Are* Humans?

Humans, both individually and collectively, are certainly the most complex thing on Earth (some say in the universe, but that is *hubris in extremis*.) Yet in our historically extremely brief time of existence, *homo sapiens* have grown sharply in numbers and accomplished quite a bit. Humans, as a species, generally think very highly of themselves. In fact, one of the things we choose to do is to subject our children to years and years of hearing about our previous accomplishments. (In truth, we should be prouder of some of these than of others.)

The Recent Growth Frame

Possibly because we see ourselves as so special, another frame in the 20th century has been as a species that continually grows—i.e., gets bigger and bigger. Continuous expansion of all things human—from population, to companies, to nations, and now to how much of the universe we live in—has become the desire of many. In this frame anything bigger—particularly involving more people and/or money—is better. Also in this frame, lack of growth is seen as a negative — stagnation. Humanity grew tremendously in the 20th century—the population quadrupled, many companies grew into enormous, worldwide entities with trillion-dollar valuations, life spans increased, and "personal growth" became a growth industry around the world.

The "Big Amoeba"

So one possible re-frame for humans and humanity in our times, that I think is already accurate, is

---

From the "best species," created from an ideal image,

To a "big destructive amoeba" starting on the planet Earth, devouring anything in its path, and looking only to grow.

That is my personal image and metaphor for this growth: a planetary-sized, shape-changing creature ("amoeba") putting out pseudopods in all directions, wanting only to grow and get bigger. This not-very-self-aware creature—i.e., humanity—is willing to eat and destroy anything in its path, including all other species of animal and plant, and even the planet's existence—in order to keep growing.

That is, I believe the frame humanity currently has.

But is that what the next generations of humans want? I believe we are just waking up to a reality that many have been happy to push aside or ignore up till now—that perpetual growth may not be the best goal for humanity, after all. Our only home planet is now undergoing significant climate change caused or at least accelerated by the human amoeba. Earth, hopefully and likely, will survive whatever comes, and will not suffer the fate of Krypton or Alderaan. But it is not clear how much of the "creature that is humanity" can, or will, survive—here, or even elsewhere. Some, like Elon Musk, are already extending new pseudopods off the Earth into space and onto other planets to find out.

A Better Frame?

Yet, in the New Age of Empowerment, I believe new frames, and new possibilities for more and better accomplishments are quickly opening up for those people who happen to be young.

The first is becoming symbiotic with our new technologies—this is, now, opening to every young person. The second comes through hacking our own biology and becoming "new humans," as Harari and others describe. This route will likely be open—at least at first—to far fewer, but could, eventually extend to all.

So Is There an Alternative Frame to the "Big Amoeba"?

My sense is that there has not yet emerged as yet a new, more positive re-frame for humanity. Today we have only the visions of either destruction on the one hand, or of the rich extending their lives and their influence over the rest on the other. That is hardly positive for all.

So perhaps it is time we got one. I suggest, and hope, it will be provided, in the New Age of Empowerment, by the newly empowered generation of people who happen to be young today.

Coalescing?

Humanity has had, up until now, a very hard time coalescing into a single cohesive unit. From its earliest beginnings It has been fragmented into countless bands, tribes, empires, nations, and thousands of affinity groups—still called "tribes" by some—based on location, interest, skin color and more. It has, at many times, and certainly today, divided into small groups of rich and large masses of poor. The idea of "earthlings"—which I have liked and identified with since I was young—exists only in science fiction.

What Is New

But one of the new and most different things about the times in which we now live is that

> *it is the very first time in the existence of humanity that people who happen to be young can communicate directly with each other—across all barriers—without the interference of the still-fragmented adults.*

It is this that leads me to my final—and aspirational—re-frame:

> *From a highly fragmented human population,*
>
> **To a single, united humanity, composed of individuals who are each unique, working together.**

One possible coming version of this is what some have called "The Hive Mind"—i.e., all people's minds connected, by technology, into a single being. Perhaps it is what Mark Zuckerberg and others mean by the Metaverse—we don't yet know.

But because we now have the first generation in the world to be connected horizontally with each other, and because people who happen to be young are just starting to understand the implications of this for themselves and what they can do—and because the technology for connection is growing so rapidly— something closer to a hive mind may be possible, even in this existing younger generation's lifetime, or the next.

We stand today on the verge of connecting all human brains and minds directly, in the Cloud. When it happens, it will be a huge re-frame for humanity, one that some currently see as positive, and others as dystopian. My own take is that humanity seeing itself as a connected whole will be very positive.

But those living in the New Age of Empowerment will surely find out. I suggest we never stop re-framing and trying on new perspectives—and, as the people who happen to be young today become more and more empowered—I hope that they, and we. Will keep on re-framing everything to better fit their New Age of Empowerment!

Harbingers

As my harbinger for the future of humanity I return, once again, to Elon Musk. My hope is that he is a harbinger of a world where humans are more connected, more imaginative, and more full of positive accomplishments. Elon has already taken many steps in these directions that show us the way—by encouraging new connections via Starlink and Neurolink, by thinking systematically and long-term by building expensive electric cars which fund mass electric cars which, in turn, fund space travel, and by leaving, via his companies, a road map to human fulfillment—i.e., sharing a big goal, loving what you do every day, and being fairly compensated. I hope we follow those maps. I have tried, here in this book, to leave one of my own.

Final Reflection Question

What are your hopes and dreams for humanity? Are humans the most important thing in the universe? Is the best solution for humanity always to keep growing? At whose expense? Will our newly empowered young people create a world that is better?

That is my hope.

Notes

1. Charles Murray, *Human Accomplishment: The Pursuit of Excellence in the Arts and Sciences, 800 B.C. to 1950*, HarperCollins 2003.
2. Thomas Kuhn, *The Structure of Scientific Revolution*, University of Chicago Press, 1962.
3. Anderson EC, Barrett LF (2016) Affective Beliefs Influence the Experience of Eating Meat. PLoS ONE 11(8): e0160424. https://doi.org/10.1371/journal.pone.0160424
4. Term from Guido van Nispen.
5. Kristof Koch, *The Quest for Consciousness: A Neurobiological Approach*, Roberts and Company, 2004.
6. Thomas Kuhn, *Op. cit.*
7. Carol Dweck, Mindset: *The New Psychology of Success*, Ballantine Books, 2006.
8. Peter Diamandis, *The Future Is Faster Than You Think*, Simon & Schuster, 2020.
9. Yuval Noah Harari, *Sapiens: A Brief History of Humankind*, Signal Books 2014.
10. Marc Prensky "Digital Natives, Digital Immigrants" originally published in *On the Horizon, 2005. Gifted; n.135 p.29-31; February 2005.*
11. John Hagel III, *The Journey Beyond Fear*, McGraw-Hill Education, 2020.
12. Andrew McAfee and Erik Brynjolfsson, *Race Against the Machine*, Digital Frontier Press, 2011.
13. RM Mayall, , Substance abuse in anaesthetists, *BJA Education*, Volume 16, Issue 7, July 2016, Pages 236–241, https://doi.org/10.1093/bjaed/mkv054
14. Term from Mark Anderson, *Strategic News Service.*
15. Alison Gopnik, *The Scientist in the Crib: What Early Learning Tells Us About the Mind*, HarperCollins, 1999.
16. Prensky, *Op. cit.*
17. Harari, *Op. cit.*
18. Name suggested by Tihana Smitran.
19. Bryan Caplan, *The Case Against Education*, Princeton University Press, 2018.
20. Harvard Medical School Dean for Medical Education Edward Hundert "tells arriving students that 'Half of what we teach you during four years of medical school is going to turn out to be wrong or irrelevant by the time you graduate.'" *Harvard Magazine*, September-October 2015.
21. Gitanjali Rao, *A Young Innovator's Guide to STEM: 5 Steps to Problem Solving for Students, Educators, and Parents*, Post Hill Press 2021.
22. Amy Morin, "4 Types of Parenting Styles and Their Effects on Kids" on Verywell Family, https://www.verywellfamily.com/ types-of-parenting-styles-1095045#\citation-1.
23. Esther Wojcicki, *How to Raise Successful People: Simple Lessons for Radical Results*, Houghton Mifflin Harcourt, 2019.
24. Alison Gopnik, *The Philosophical Baby: What Children's Minds Tell Us About Truth, Love and the Meaning of Life*, Farrar, Straus & Giroux, 2009.
25. Will Durant, The Greatest Minds and Ideas of All Time (complied by John Little), Simon & Schuster, 2002.
26. Michael M. Crow, talk at ASU/GSV, 2021.
27. James Paul Gee, *What is a Human?: Language, Mind and Culture*, Palgrave Macmillan 2020.
28. Yuval Noah Harari, *Op. cit.*

About the Author

MARC PRENSKY is an internationally acclaimed keynote speaker and author. The gold-prize-winning author of 10 books, he has given talks in over 40 countries. Marc is the coiner of the globally recognized term "digital native." He serves on the Advisory Boards of several organizations. Marc recently founded the *Two Billion Kids Project* (twobillionkids.org), and the *Global Ministry of Empowerment Accomplishment and Impact (ministry-of-eai.org).*

Marc can be contacted at marcprensky@gmail.com.

Additional Resources

More related to empowerment, including lists of completed projects by young people of all ages, can be found at:

https://Ministry-of-eai.org

https://Btwdatabase.org

https://PlanetPilots.org

https://DFCworld.com

Recommended books:

Digital Natives Rising
Ourboox online, 2021
bit.ly/digital-natives-rising

Empowerment Today!
Ourboox online, 2021
bit.ly/empowerment-today

A Young Innovator's Guide to STEM:
5 Steps to Problem Solving for Students, Educators, and Parents
by Gitanjali Rao, Post Hill Press 2021

Danielle, Chronicles of a Superheroine
by Ray Kurzweil, WordFire Press, 2019